COMPETITIVE SWIMMING
FOR NEW CHAMPIONS

COMPETITIVE SWIMMING FOR NEW CHAMPIONS

A Guide to the Kinesthetic Feedback Approach

by DR. DON VAN ROSSEN and BARBARA WOODRICH

Illustrated by TOM KELLY
Photographs by ANDY WHIPPLE

NEW YORK • ST. LOUIS • SAN FRANCISCO • AUCKLAND
DÜSSELDORF • JOHANNESBURG • BOGOTÁ • LONDON
MADRID • MEXICO • MONTREAL • NEW DELHI • PANAMA
PARIS • SÃO PAULO • SINGAPORE • SYDNEY • TOKYO •
TORONTO

Library of Congress Cataloging in Publication Data

Van Rossen, Don.
  Competitive swimming for young champions.

  SUMMARY: Discusses preparation for competitive swimming, including drills, diet, rest, and attitudes.
  Includes index.
  1. Swimming for children—Juvenile literature. [1. Swimming] I. Woodrich, Barbara, joint author. II. Kelly, Tom, 1943–   III. Whipple, Andy. IV. Title.
GV837.2.V38   797.2′1   78–7603
ISBN 0–07–071690–0

Design by Jean Krulis

To the memory of
COACH MAC NAKANO
and
To LEIGH DEAN
who made a dream a reality
_____

Contents

Foreword /   10

Prologue / THE RACE   13

    One / YOUR BODY IN WATER   19

    Two / LEARN YOUR BEST NATURAL STROKES
        WITH DRILLS   36

    Three / DRILLS FOR THE FRONT CRAWL   41

    Four / DRILLS FOR THE BACKSTROKE   50

    Five / DRILLS FOR THE BREASTSTROKE   60

    Six / DRILLS FOR THE BUTTERFLY   70

    Seven / STARTS   83

    Eight / TURNS   103

    Nine / WATER TRAINING   120

    Ten / DRY LAND TRAINING   131

    Eleven / PREPARING FOR COMPETITION   147

    Twelve / THE SWIM MEET   159

    Thirteen / WHAT MAKES A SUCCESSFUL SWIMMER? 169

    / SWIM TEAM VOCABULARY   175

    / INDEX   185

FOREWORD

Have you ever wondered if there is a more efficient and faster way of swimming your strokes in competition? There is! Every human body is unique in bone density, muscle weight, alignment of skeletal parts, and degree of flexibility. There is a natural stroke for each swimmer.

Teachers and coaches of swimming are discovering new techniques for teaching natural strokes. Rather than using eyes and ears to send instructions to the muscles, they are using muscles to send messages to the brain. This teaching method is called *movement sensitization.*

The drills presented in this book fit together to develop natural strokes for each swimmer. They are designed to produce stroke techniques that are relaxed, rhythmic, and balanced. They are an effective approach for teaching and training all levels of competitive swimmers.

This method was used at a summer sports camp. Nearly two hundred boys and girls from eight to seventeen were coached during six one-week periods. The group ranged in ability from novices to several swimmers whose times ranked in the top ten nationally.

The swimmers were timed for 50 yards of each stroke on the first day of training. For the next 4½ days, they began each morning with running—building up to 3½ miles by the end of the week. They spent a minimum of six hours daily in the water working only on drills. Another thirty to forty-five minutes were spent working on land exercises.

One would expect that the extreme activity would have built up a high degree of fatigue in these swimmers. However, when they were timed again at the end of the week, 89 percent of the times had improved. And the majority of the swimmers swam lifetime best times. The percentage of improved times held true for each of the six one-week sessions.

The drills have been enthusiastically accepted by men's and women's swim teams at the University of Oregon and have been used in their training to improve performances. They have also been successfully used as a teaching method in university classes.

When teaching and training in a competitive program are divided into two separate phases, there is often too little time spent on improving skills. Coaches tend to pass quickly through the teaching phase to push for the high level of fitness swimmers need for competition.

By using the drills in this book, teaching and training can be combined. Swimmers will not lose the quality of speed and efficiency if they learn to feel their natural strokes.

DR. DON VAN ROSSEN

PROLOGUE/THE RACE

"SWIMMERS UP!"

A hush falls over the crowd that fills the bleachers. The finals of the state age-group outdoor championship meet are about to begin. All eyes turn to the participants in the opening event—a 100-meter freestyle race.

Six sun-tanned swimmers climb onto the starting blocks at the end of the pool. They shake their arms and legs and breathe deeply.

"TAKE YOUR MARKS!"

As the starter raises his gun, the swimmers curl into their starting positions—toes over the edge of the block, knees bent, heads and arms hanging down loosely.

Bang!

At the sound of the gun, they uncoil and shoot forward. Outstretched bodies hit the smooth surface like skipping stones and break it into a splash. Then arms and legs churn the water as they push the swimmers rapidly down the pool. All six reach the end wall and flip nearly at the same time.

As they start their second length, Pat, swimming in Lane 3, has taken the lead, with Terry, in Lane 4, close behind. They pull hard down the pool and flip again. Pat's lead has widened and the swimmers in the outside lanes have fallen behind until the six competitors resemble the formation of a flock of geese in flight.

Suddenly, with a burst of speed, Terry begins to close the gap and finally catches the leader at the end of the pool. The two flip together and match stroke for stroke as they race to the finish. As they touch the wall, neither knows who has won. It is so close that only the electronic timer, which will give times to a hundredth of a second, can name the winner.

Pat and Terry turn to look up at the reader board as the rest of the swimmers race to the wall. Bright lights flash the message. Terry, in Lane 4, is in first place with a time of 59.82. Pat is a very close second with 59.83.

Pat shakes Terry's hand. "Good swim! But watch out for me next meet!"

"Thanks! Guess I had a little bit of luck. That's my best time ever!"

"A little bit of luck and a big bit of work. I know! It's the first time I've broken a minute, too."

"Hey, that's great! We're on our way! Right?"

"Right!"

"MAY I HAVE YOUR ATTENTION, PLEASE?"

The roar of the cheering crowd fades at the sound of the announcer's voice over the loudspeaker.

"WE HAVE A NEW STATE RECORD OF 59.82 IN THE 100-METER FREESTYLE . . ."

The swimmers in the other lanes dive under the lane lines and surface in Lane 4.

"Way to go, Terry!"

"Congratulations!"

"A 59.82! That's great!"

"And a state record, no less!"

There is laughter and handshaking as the swimmers congratulate one another. To have made the finals in the state championship meet is a feat of which all can be proud. They are the top swimmers in their age group. They have trained hard for a long time to reach the top and have had many disappointments along the way. They have learned to be good winners and good losers.

All of these swimmers are champions. Would *you* like to be a champion swimmer? If you would, it is important that you have a good understanding of your body and how you can best use it in the water.

COMPETITIVE SWIMMING
FOR NEW CHAMPIONS

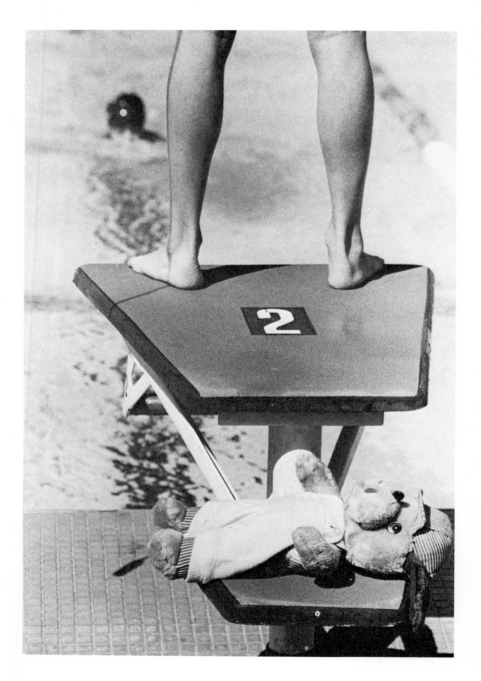

Chapter One

YOUR BODY IN WATER

Your body is different from any other body in the world. It has its own strengths and weaknesses, its own advantages and disadvantages. By understanding your body, you can discover how to move through the water with the greatest ease and speed for the energy you use. When you perfect your own natural strokes, none of your energy will be wasted. All of it can be used to help you swim faster.

Some things that are important in swimming, such as flexibility and strength, can be improved with proper exercise. A later chapter will describe exercises that will improve your flexibility and strength. Other things, such as bone density and buoyancy, cannot be changed. However, you can adjust your style of swimming to make the most of your natural advantages and minimize your disadvantages.

You may find that your body is much better suited to one stroke than another. Or you may excel in distance swimming even though you do not do well in short sprints. By knowing your body and how it can best be used in the water, you will be able to make the most of your natural strengths and learn how to overcome your weaknesses.

There are tests you can use to help you understand your own body in water. At the beginning of the season enter the results of the tests for flexibility and strength on your PERSONAL PROFILE chart. Record the results of these same tests again at midseason and finally at the end of the season. Your PERSONAL PROFILE will help you and your coach decide what strokes and distances will be best for you. This record will also be valuable in coming seasons to help you chart your progress from year to year.

TESTS FOR FLEXIBILITY

SHOULDER FLEXIBILITY

Shoulder flexibility is most important for the backstroke and butterfly. It has some advantage for freestyle but is not essential.

To test your shoulder flexibility, stand with both arms extended in front of you at shoulder height. Keep your palms down and move your hands back until they are as far behind you as possible. They should remain at shoulder level.

Pretend you are standing in the center of a clock looking at 12:00. If you can bring your arms back to the 4:00 and 8:00 positions, your flexibility is average. Anything beyond 5:00 and 7:00 is excellent.

ANKLE EXTENSION

Ankle extension is most important in the flutter kick for

PERSONAL PROFILE FOR _____ Your Name

	SHOULDER FLEXIBILITY		ANKLE EXTENSION		ANKLE FLECTION		HIP-AND-ANKLE ROTATION		STRENGTH		BUOYANCY
	part of season— start mid end		part of season— start mid end		part of season— start mid end		part of season— start mid end		part of season— start mid end		no change
EXCELLENT											
GOOD											
AVERAGE											
BELOW AVERAGE											
POOR											

the front and back crawl and in the dolphin kick for the butterfly.

To test your ankle extension flexibility, sit on the floor or pool deck with your legs extended in front of you and the backs of your knees touching the floor or deck. Point your toes as hard as you can and push them toward the floor without lifting your knees. How far are your toes from the floor? Three inches or less shows excellent ankle extension flexibility (Fig. 1).

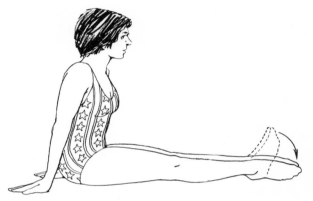

Fig. 1 / Ankle Extension.

ANKLE FLECTION

Ankle flection is important for developing a strong breast-stroke kick.

To test your ankle flection, stand up, then bend your knees until you are sitting in a squatting position (Fig. 2). If you can stay in this position for ten seconds without lifting your heels from the deck, you have enough ankle flexibility for a good breaststroke kick.

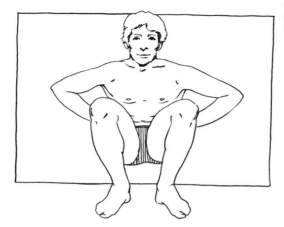

Fig. 2 / Ankle Flection.

HIP-AND-ANKLE ROTATION

Hip-and-ankle rotation is also important if you hope to develop a strong breaststroke kick.

To test your flexibility in hip-and-ankle rotation, lie on your stomach on the floor or pool deck with your toes pointed out (Fig. 3).

Fig. 3 / Hip-and-Ankle Rotation.

Can you touch the inside of your foot to the floor or deck? If you can, you have the hip-and-ankle rotation needed for a powerful breaststroke kick.

TEST FOR STRENGTH

POOL PUSH-OUT

Strength in shoulders and arms is very important for all four competitive strokes. Test yourself by trying a Pool Push-Out.

Start in a vertical position with the front of your body touching the side of the pool. Your hands should be flat on the pool deck above the gutter. Your fingertips should point straight ahead. Press down until you bring your body up and out of the water with your arms extended at your sides. Don't

Fig. 4 / Pool Push-Out.

push off the bottom with your feet! Your arms should do all the work (Fig. 4).

If you can't do a Pool Push-Out on the first try, don't be discouraged. Your strength will increase with land exercises.

TESTS FOR BUOYANCY

How buoyant are you? Swimmers who are naturally buoyant have an advantage because it is easier for them to swim in a horizontal position. A horizontal position creates less resistance and helps you move through the water with the greatest speed and the least expenditure of energy.

ONE-IN-A-MILLION TEST

Occasionally we find a person who is extremely buoyant. Only one person in a million or more has this gift, but those who do have an exceptional advantage as swimmers. Are you one of those people? Try this test.

Take a deep breath and curl into a tuck float position. Your head should be on your chest and your arms wrapped around your legs. Now exhale *all* the air in your lungs. If you are like most of us, you will gradually sink to the bottom. If you remain floating, you're one of the few fortunate people with the gift of exceptional buoyancy.

ANGLE-OF-FLOTATION TEST

You can test your degree of buoyancy by your angle of flotation. In a front float, your body will settle at an angle that will show your natural buoyancy.

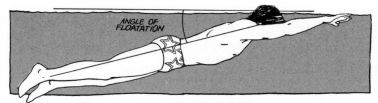

Fig. 5 / Angle-of-Flotation Test.

Float on your stomach, sculling to keep your head above the water. Have a partner hold your ankles lightly just under the surface. Now take a deep breath and put your face in the water. Stretch your arms over your head and press them tightly against your ears. Tuck your chin down to your chest. Your partner should gently release your ankles and let your legs settle to your natural angle of flotation (Fig. 5).

If you are floating with your feet close to the surface, you are very buoyant. Most people will float with some degree of angle. A swimmer with the least buoyancy will float in a nearly vertical position.

HOW TO COMPENSATE FOR LACK OF BUOYANCY

Are you an angle floater or a vertical floater? Don't despair! Not all champion swimmers are buoyant. You can compensate for a lack of buoyancy and still keep your body in a horizontal position as you swim.

DEVELOP A STRONG KICK
A strong, steady kick will help keep your body horizontal as well as provide power to move you forward.

BALANCE YOUR LEGS BY LOWERING THE POSITION OF YOUR HEAD

Your body behaves much like a teeter-totter, with your hips as the center. When you are in a prone float position and lift your head, your legs will sink. Lowering your head and looking at the bottom of the pool instead of ahead as you swim will help keep your body horizontal.

You can feel the importance of your head position if you try this exercise.

First, swim a front crawl with your head above the water.

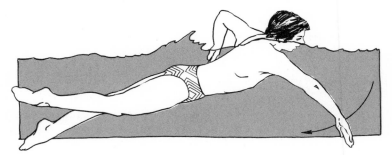

Fig. 6 / Balance Your Legs by Lowering the Position of Your Head. (a) Head above water. (b) Chin tucked down on chest.

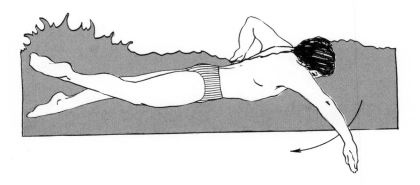

Feel your legs sink? The angle of your body is resisting the water and making it harder for you to move ahead. You must press down on the water as well as pull back and you must kick hard just to keep from sinking. This is wasted energy.

Now tuck your chin down on your chest. Feel your legs rise? Your horizontal position now offers minimal resistance. Your pull and kick will move you forward with much less effort (Fig. 6).

The teeter-totter principle applies to your arms as well as your head. In swimming the butterfly, your legs will tend to sink as your arms come close to your sides but will rise as your arms are extended.

SPEED, OR HYDROPLANING

Sprint, or short-distance, swimmers can counteract a lack of buoyancy with speed. They lift their heads and look forward. Their heads then act like the tips of water skis, lifting them to the top of the water. They ride high for the same reason that a water skier stays on the surface of the water—because they are moving fast (Fig. 7).

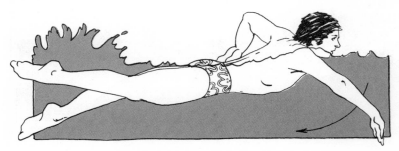

Fig. 7 / Hydroplaning.

EXPLOSIVE BREATHING

Buoyancy can also be improved by explosive breathing. Instead of gradually exhaling, swimmers hold air in their lungs until they are ready to breathe again. The air is then quickly expelled and another breath is taken and held.

MORE FACTS ABOUT YOUR BODY IN WATER

You have learned how swimming in a horizontal position helps your body move through the water with maximum speed and minimum effort. But there are other factors that will affect the movement of your body through the water.

PROPELLING FORCES

Your hands and feet act as paddles to push you through the water. In order to make the best use of these paddles, you must use the greatest possible surface area to push against the water.

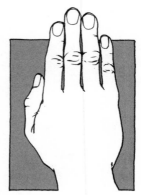

HANDS. Lay your hands flat on the surface of the pool deck. Your thumbs should be held next to your fingers, and your fingers should be together and flat—but also relaxed. This is the best position for swimming because it creates the widest paddle to push the water (Fig. 8).

Fig. 8 / Propelling Forces. Hands.

FEET.   To feel the best position for your feet in a flutter kick or dolphin kick, lie on your stomach on the pool deck. Press the tops of your feet down so that as much of your foot as possible is in contact with the deck. Your toes will be pointed and your feet will be slightly pigeon-toed. This position gives you the flattest surface for pushing against the water (Fig. 9).

Fig. 9   /   Propelling Forces. Feet.

LINE OF FORCE

We often think that the arms in the front crawl are traveling in a circle. To get the greatest force from your arm movement, however, your arms should travel not in a circle

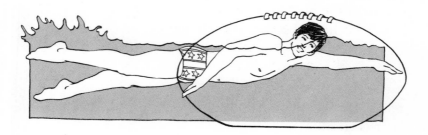

Fig. 10   /   Line of Force.

like a basketball but rather like a football that is flat on the bottom. Your hands should travel in as long a line as possible. The longer the pull, the more speed you will get for your energy (Fig. 10).

To practice your freestyle pull, stretch a rope beneath you about a foot below the surface of the water. This can be done by bending two strips of metal (a welder may have to help with this) until they fit snugly over the lip of the pool gutter. Drill a hole in each metal strip about a foot below the surface of the water and fit an eye bolt into each hole. Screw the nuts on tightly, and saw off any of the bolt that protrudes beyond the nut. Place the two strips on opposite sides of the pool. Then put a rope through each eye bolt and draw it tight.

Fig. 11 / Using a Rope to
Practice Freestyle Pull.

Now, grab the rope and pull yourself forward. This is the path your hand should travel (Fig. 11).

If you cannot make the metal strips, or if your pool does not have a gutter, try to imagine the rope beneath the water and make your hands follow that line.

position for another kick or pull is called the *recovery*. The recovery is the rest phase of the stroke. It provides a balance with the propelling, or work, phase.

In strokes such as the front crawl and backstroke, the propelling arm alternates with the recovering arm. In an alternating arm action, it takes skill and practice to train the recovering arm to relax while the propelling arm pulls.

Chapter Two

LEARN YOUR BEST NATURAL STROKES WITH DRILLS

It's 6:30 A.M. The sun paints the clouds in the eastern sky pink and gold as it peeks over the hills. Young swimmers in tight-fitting nylon suits come out of their dressing rooms. They check the bulletin board for warm-up instructions for their group, then head for the pool, from which a cloud of steam rises into the chill morning air.

Group III's instructions read: KICK 20, PULL 20, SWIM 20. Each swimmer takes a styrofoam kickboard from a pile, dives into an outside lane and begins kicking down the pool with the board held out in front at arm's length. In two of the four center lanes, Group II swimmers are pulling. Their legs are supported by plastic floats. Group I swimmers, the oldest and fastest, are in the other two center lanes. Each swimmer is swimming laps, using the stroke he or she most often swims in competition.

Group IV swimmers, the youngest and beginning competitors, are kicking lengths in the other two outside lanes. They will begin with a shorter warm-up, but most, with time and practice, will move to Group III, to Group II, and finally to the longest warm-up with Group I.

After the warm-up, the coach conducts the training session. Swimmers are asked to repeat a series of twenty 100-meter swims of 4 lengths of the 25-meter pool where this team trains. Between each swim, they rest for fifteen seconds.

At other times in the season, the coach may ask them to repeat swims of 50 meters (2 lengths) or 200 meters (8 lengths), and the rest periods between may be shorter or longer. Repeating a set distance with a set rest period between each swim is called *interval training.* The coach will use interval training to work on all four competitive strokes: front crawl, backstroke, breaststroke, and butterfly.

Swim team practices similar to this are taking place once or twice a day in pools around the world. They may be held in indoor or outdoor pools, sponsored by YM/YWCA's, boys' clubs, Jewish community centers, park and recreation areas, private clubs, or schools.

Thousands of young people from six to seventeen participate in the age-group swimming program governed by the Amateur Athletic Union (AAU). Swimmers are divided into six age groups: eight and under, nine and ten, eleven and twelve, thirteen and fourteen, fifteen through seventeen, and senior. Anyone twelve or over may participate in the senior division. Because it is an open competition for all quality athletes, it offers the greatest competitive challenge.

It is easier to become a champion swimmer if you can join a swim team. If you live in a large city, there will probably be several teams in your area. If you are from a small town, there may be only one team, or there may be a number of teams in a larger town nearby. The competition in your practice sessions, the team spirit in swim meets, and the helpful instruction of a good coach will all contribute to your success.

A good coach knows the basics of competitive swimming and understands young people. He or she should also recognize the unique aptitudes of each swimmer. One way coaches can help team members develop their best strokes is through drills designed to help each swimmer feel the results of his or her own movements.

USING THE DRILLS

Because your body is unique, you must find the way that it can best be used to propel you through the water with the greatest ease and speed for the amount of energy you expend. The drills in the following chapters will help you find the most efficient ways of using your arms, legs, and body position. They will help you polish your swimming techniques, and they will increase your speed.

Your muscles will begin to be sensitized in the first 50 yards of each drill. That is, they will act as messengers to let you know how they can best work for you. This is a learning process to help you find your best natural stroke. For this learning to become a habit, you should practice 50 yards or meters of each drill at least three times during a practice session three or more times a week.

After the drills are learned, they can be used in training to polish techniques and increase speed. They should be repeated in 50- to 100-meter intervals for 800 meters or more, depending on you age and ability. Since most training pools are 25 meters or yards long, this will mean 16 times 2 lengths, or 8 times 4 lengths. If you train in a 50-meter pool, swim 1 length 16 times, or 2 lengths 8 times, with a short rest between each swim.

In a training program, different goals are stressed in preseason training than in the competitive, or championship, part of the season. The GUIDE FOR WATER TRAINING chart (see page 125) will help you understand the progression of training during the season. In early training, you should give particular attention to learning the skills you will need in competition and to developing the strokes that are best for you. In the early competitive season, training is designed to polish your techniques, while in the championship season, speed is stressed. Each drill is coded to indicate its use in any or all phases of training: L = learning, T = polishing techniques, S = increasing speed. The drills coded L would be best used in preseason, those coded S are better for the competitive season, while those coded T fit well into all phases of training. And those drills coded X are best suited to experienced competitive swimmers. Unless your strokes are at a high skill level, your muscles will not give you the best feedback with the X-coded drills.

Some of the drills have particular importance for resensitizing your muscles to your best natural stroke. These drills should be used for a warm-up at the beginning of each practice and before each meet. After the drills for each stroke, you will find a suggested series of warm-up drills.

SWIM TEAM VOCABULARY

There are some words and expressions used often in competitive swimming which may not be familiar to you. If you find a word or expression you do not understand, turn to the SWIM TEAM VOCABULARY (page 175) for a definition.

Chapter Three

DRILLS FOR THE FRONT CRAWL

You will find that the front crawl is the fastest and most popular way of moving through the water. Because there are more competitors in the front crawl, or freestyle, events, qualifying times are more difficult to make.

You will do most of your training with the front crawl because it is the most efficient stroke for long distances and because there are more events in that stroke than in the others. This does not mean, however, that you will necessarily swim the front crawl in competition.

In competition, your kick becomes more important. You will need it, as well as your arms, to push you faster through the water. You will also need to increase the RPM, or revolutions per minute, of both your arms and legs. The drills will not only help you find your own strokes but will improve your competitive speed by increasing your RPM and making you more aware of your kick.

As you swim the front crawl, your arms will move in a balanced, steady, circular motion. One hand will reach forward, or recover, above the water while the other hand pulls beneath the water. The pattern your arms should make is much like a football that is flat on the bottom. This will give you a long, straight *line of force.* You should throw the water back with increasing speed and *follow through.* At the end of

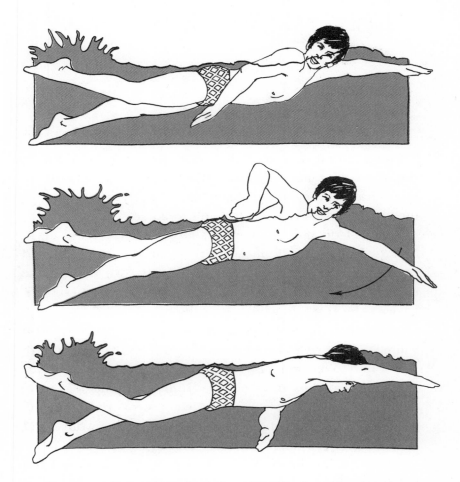

Fig. 14 / Front Crawl. (a, b, c, and d) show circular arm motion, flutter-kick leg motion, and breathing motion of the head.

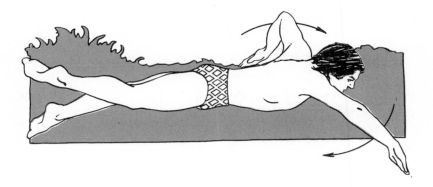

each pull, throw the water toward your feet so that the *direction of force* will move your body forward.

You must concentrate on a powerful, controlled kick that you can feel pushing your body through the water. Your legs will move in an up-and-down motion called a flutter kick. Kick one foot and then the other from your hips, with your knees and ankles relaxed. Your toes should be pointed and a little pigeon-toed.

You can breathe by turning your head to the side just as your hand on that side goes past your leg. Take a breath, turn your face back into the water, and hold the air in your lungs until you are ready to breathe again. Explode the air out before taking your next breath (Fig. 14).

DRILLS FOR FINDING YOUR OWN STROKE

In school, most knowledge comes to you through your eyes and ears. You learn by listening and seeing. These drills will help you learn not only through your eyes and ears but through your muscles, which will feel what movements are most natural and give you the greatest speed through the water.

Think of your feet. Does a deeper or shallower kick feel best? Think of your hands. Feel them control the water to push you forward. Let your mind and body work together as you use the drills to find your own natural stroke.

Drill 1—Silent Kick L, T, S

Hold a kickboard at arm's length in front of you, and kick silently so that your heels ripple the water but do not break the surface. Your kick will be narrow, your toes pointed. The narrow, silent kick will help you control your legs in a sprint swim.

Drill 2—Boiling-Water Kick L

Kick hard, allowing your feet to break the surface of the water and make a big churning behind you as you go. This kick will be deeper than the silent one. It will give you support and propulsion with a little less effort.

Which kick felt more comfortable to you? Which made you go faster? There may be a kick somewhere between these two that will work best with your arm stroke. Find the kick that is right for *you!*

Drill 3—Scooter With Silent Kick L, T, S

Hold a kickboard in front of you on the surface of the water under your left arm. Pull with your right arm for one length of the pool. Then switch the board to your right arm and pull another length with your left. Kick with a silent kick. Keep your kick and your arms moving steadily. Both your arms and your legs are working together to push you through the water. Find the *balance* that makes neither your arms nor your legs get too tired. Increase the speed of your hand as you pull and push toward your feet and follow through (Fig. 15).

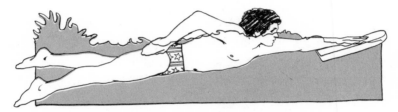

Fig. 15 / Scooter with Silent Kick. Drill 3.

Drill 4—Scooter With Boiling-Water Kick L
Pull as in Drill 3, but use a deep boiling-water kick as in Drill 2.

Drill 5—Scooter With Your Best Kick
Pull as in Drills 3 and 4, but use the kick that feels best with your arm stroke. Think of pulling the same path that you pulled holding the rope. Pull your body over and past your hand. Throw the water in a straight *line of force* toward your

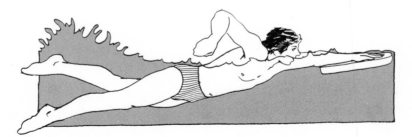

Fig. 16 / Scooter with Your Best Kick. Drill 5.

feet. Accelerate the speed of your hand, and follow through at the end of your stroke (Fig. 16).

Drill 6—Crossover Pulling L, T

Swim with your pull alone by holding a support between your legs. Pull so that your arms cross over each other and each hand is pulling beneath the opposite shoulder. As you pull, point each thumb toward the surface of the water like the periscope of a submarine. Feel your body lean into your stroke? You are using your body to *transfer momentum* to your arms (Fig. 17).

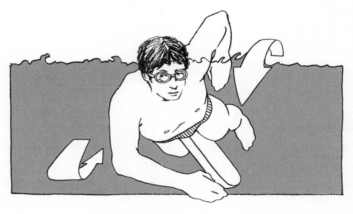

Fig. 17 / Crossover Pulling. Drill 6. Note: Goggles protect eyes from chlorine and increase visibility.

Drill 7—Front Crawl With Crossover Pulling L, T

Swim the front crawl with both arms, and kick. Cross over your arm as you pull (as in Drill 6). Feel how easily your arms can start your body moving forward? This pull can often be effective for distance swimmers or swimmers with below-average arm and shoulder strength. How does it feel to you?

Drill 8—Hydroplane T, S

Do the front crawl with a silent kick, holding your breath as long as you can. Look forward, and keep the water line just above your eyes. Feel your kick push you through the water. You will ride high in the water like a hydroplane.

DRILLS TO REFINE YOUR STROKE

Drills 1–8 have helped you find your best natural stroke. How does it feel? It should be balanced and fluid. Feel your body move the water? If your stroke is natural, you will be relaxed. All parts of your body will work together. Now you are ready to refine and tune up your natural stroke for the greatest possible speed.

Some of the drills may emphasize *overloading*. When you carry a stack of heavy books up the stairs, your legs are overloaded and must work harder. If you do this many times, it will be much easier to run upstairs without your heavy burden. Similarly, your strokes will seem easier after you have practiced the overloading drills.

Drill 9—Head Above Water T, S, X

Swim the front crawl with your head above the water. This will overload your stroke. In this position, you must kick and pull harder and faster to move forward. As you kick hard and pull with a long stroke, you should feel you are lifting your body and swimming high in the water.

Drill 10—Build-Up Swims T, S

Swim your whole front crawl stroke, but . . .

A. THINK KICK! Think of your kick pushing you through the water.

B. THINK PULL! Continue to kick, but think of your arms pulling hard.

C. THINK KICK AND PULL! Think of your kick pushing and your arms pulling.

D. THINK SPEED! Build up speed. Kick and pull harder and faster. Think of riding on top of the water. Make your body a hydroplane.

WARM-UP DRILLS

At the beginning of each practice session and before every swim meet, resensitize your muscles with a warm-up drill for the front crawl. Swim one length of the pool with each of these drills: Drill 1—Silent Kicking, Drill 3—Scooter with Silent Kick, Drill 7—Front Crawl with Crossover Pulling, and Drill 8—Hydroplane (beginners and intermediates), or Drill 9—Head Above Water (experienced only). Finish tuning up your muscles with Drill 10, swimming one length each of Build-Up Swims A through D.

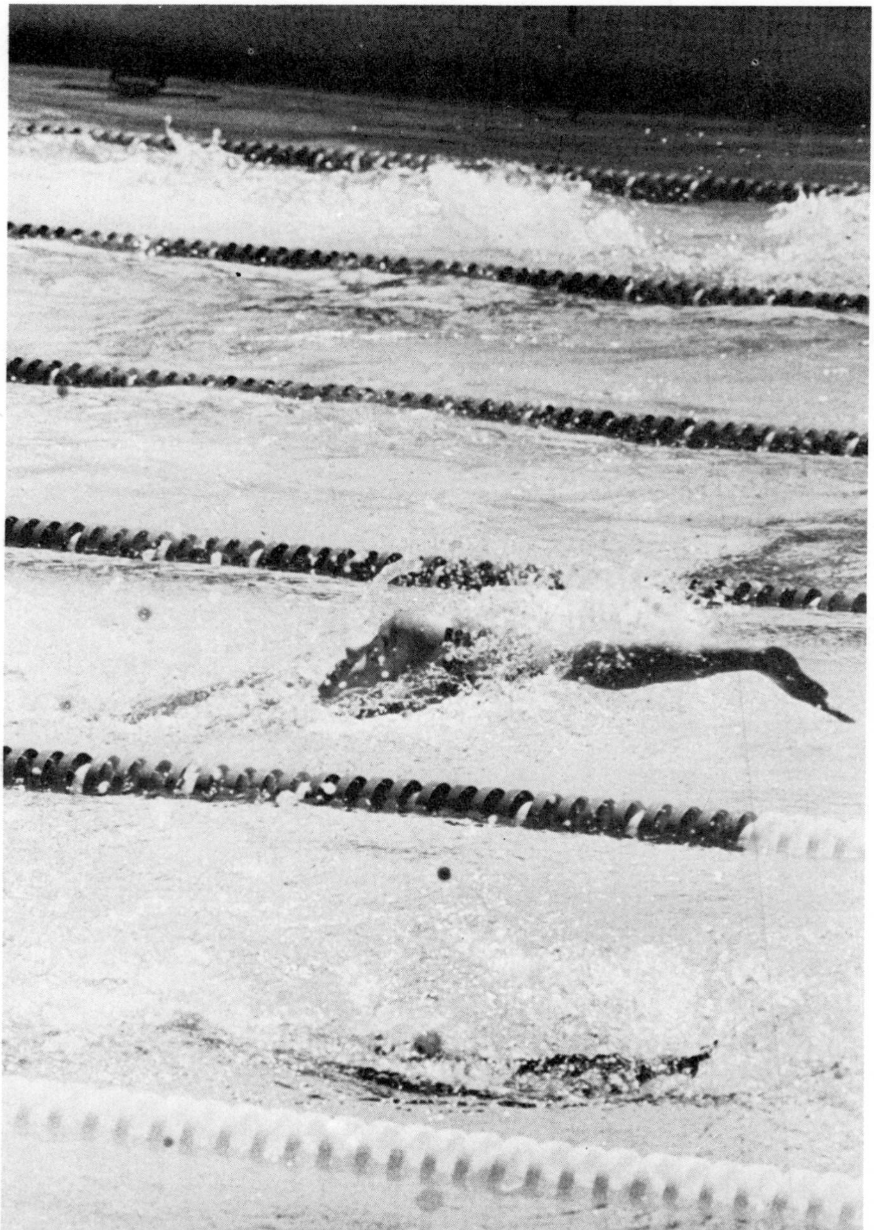

Chapter Four

DRILLS FOR THE BACKSTROKE

In the back crawl, or backstroke, you will again be swimming with your arms traveling in a balanced, steady, circular motion. One hand will pull beneath the water while the other recovers above the water. Your pull should closely follow a straight line. Your elbows will bend as your hand throws the water toward your feet. Your arms and shoulders should be relaxed as you recover.

Your legs will move in very nearly the same up-and-down flutter-kick action you used in the front crawl, but your toes will be more pointed. Your kick will feel much like the silent kicking drill you practiced for your front crawl stroke. Again, you will try to keep your body stretched and flat to offer the least resistance to the water.

Since your face remains out of the water, breathing is easy, but most backstrokers take a breath while recovering their right arm. Explosive breathing will help you ride higher in the water.

DRILLS FOR FINDING YOUR OWN STROKE

As you practice the following drills, remember to let your mind and body work together. Be sensitive to the messages your muscles are sending. Feel your rhythm, balance, and body position. Are your feet and hands propelling you with ease and speed?

Unless you are an experienced competitive swimmer, some of the drills may seem difficult at first. Don't despair! Remember, the more you practice, the easier they will become.

Drill 1—Sit And Kick L, T

Hold a kickboard by putting your arms across the top the way you might put them across the top of your desk at school. Sit in the water with your hips aligned under your shoulders and your legs extended in front of you. Kick so that you break the surface of the water and throw the water

Fig. 18 / Sit and Kick. Drill 1.

off your toes. The sitting position will stretch your ankles. What part of the kick propels you backward? (Fig. 18.)

Drill 2—Kick And Count L, T

Kick on your back with your hands at your sides. Your legs and ankles should be relaxed. Again, throw the water off your toes. Count every three kicks—1, 2, 3, 1, 2, 3—three kicks while your right arm pulls, then three kicks while your left arm pulls. This kick pattern gives rhythm and balance to your stroke.

Drill 3—Kickboard Over Knees L

Hold a kickboard at arm's length over your knees on the surface of the water as you kick. This will help you remember to kick your whole leg. Your knees will not break the surface of the water. Your feet must do most of the work (Fig. 19).

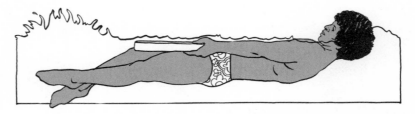

Fig. 19 / Kickboard over Knees. Drill 3.

Drill 4—Kickboard Over Head L, T, S

Hold a kickboard at arm's length on the surface of the water above your head as you kick. Stretch your body to make it streamlined and straight as an arrow. This is your natural body position for the backstroke. Kick hard so that you are riding high in the water (Fig. 20).

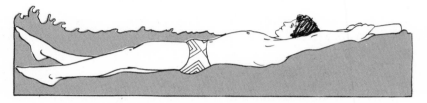

Fig. 20 / Kickboard over Head. Drill 4.

Drill 5—Hands Locked Over Head L, T, S, X

Lock your hands together and keep your arms straight above your head as you kick. You will feel stretched and streamlined. Kick hard and fast. Try dropping your chin to your chest. If you are kicking fast, your head will lift you higher in the water like the tip of a water ski.

Drill 6—One-Arm Swim L, T

Hold one arm at your side and pull with the other. Continue to kick. Catch the water with your hand and throw it in a straight *line of force* toward your feet. How much must

Fig. 21 / One-Arm Swim. Drill 6.

you bend your elbow so that your hand can move in a straight line? Use your right arm alone for one length of the pool, then your left arm for another length. If your body wiggles, you're not throwing straight! Don't try to pull too deep! (Fig. 21)

Drill 7—Rowboat L, T

Pull with both arms moving together like the oars of a rowboat. Both hands will reach back together. Then both hands will throw the water toward your feet. Again, both elbows must bend to pull a straight line. Keep your kick strong and your body stretched and streamlined (Fig. 22).

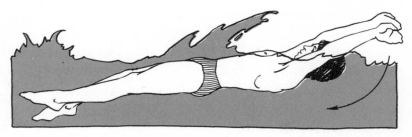

Fig. 22 / Rowboat. Drill 7.

Drill 8—Cymbals L, T, S

Pull with both arms moving together like the oars of a rowboat as in Drill 7. This time, clap your hands on your thighs as they brush by and then together above your hips before you reach back for another pull. Your hands should make a continuous circle and follow through.

Drill 9—Shark L, T

Hold a kickboard between your legs and pull with a back crawl arm stroke. One arm should be pulling beneath the water while the other arm recovers above the water (Fig. 23).

Fig. 23 / Shark. Drill 9.

Try to keep the board between your legs from twisting or wobbling. Make it move in a straight line like a shark's fin.

To keep the board steady, your pull must be balanced and your hands must move in a straight line. How much do you need to bend your elbows?

DRILLS TO REFINE YOUR STROKE

Drills 1–9 have helped you find your own natural backstroke. Is your body stretched and long from the tips of your fingers to the tips of your toes? Are your arms light and high as they recover? Can you feel your hands grabbing handfuls of water and throwing it toward your toes? Your body should feel light and high in the water. Now you are ready to refine and tune up your backstroke for speed.

Drill 10—Waiter Kick L, T

Hold a kickboard like a waiter's tray above your chest with both hands while you kick on your back. Hold it high. You will have to kick hard and fast to stay high in the water.

Drill 11—Water-Ski Jump L, T, S, X

Hold one arm out of the water like a water-ski jump. Your hand should be above your hips and your arm at a 45-degree angle to the surface. Pull with the other hand. Pull a length of the pool with your right arm, then a length with your left. Keep kicking! Your toes should still be continuously breaking the surface of the water. This will help you feel the balance of kick to pull and the amount of kick necessary to move you through the water for speed swimming (Fig. 24).

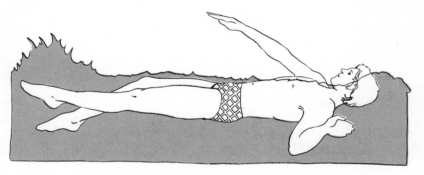

Fig. 24 / Water-Ski Jump. Drill 11.

Drill 12—Cup Of Water L, T

See if you can swim a length of the pool while balancing an imaginary cup of water on your forehead. Feel how steady your head must be!

Drill 13—Shoulder Shrug L, T

To get a relaxed recovery, let your shoulder lead your arm. Shrug your shoulder as if you were pulling your arm out of a sleeve. Or rotate your arm so that your elbow points toward the sky. Keep your arm high while you reach back for another pull. This will allow your arm to rest while your shoulder does the work (Fig. 25).

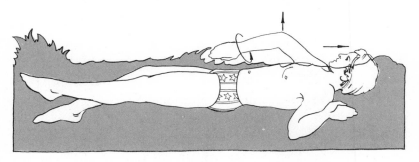

Fig. 25 / Shoulder Shrug. Drill 13.

Drill 14—Stretch And Streamline L, T, S

Swim long! Stretch your body and make it as long and streamlined as you can. Keep your toes pointed, your feet long. Reach to the sky when you recover your arms.

Drill 15—Build-Up Swims T, S

Swim your whole back crawl stroke, but . . .

A. THINK KICK! Think of your kick pushing you through the water. Throw the water off your toes.

B. THINK PULL! Keep your kick continuous, but think of your hands throwing the water toward your toes.

C. THINK KICK, PULL, AND STRETCH! Think of your kick

pushing, your arms throwing, your body stretched and streamlined.

D. THINK SPEED! Build up speed. Kick and pull harder and faster. Think of riding on the water. Tuck your chin down and be a hydroplane.

WARM-UP DRILLS

At the beginning of each practice session and before every swim meet, resensitize your muscles with a warm-up drill for the backstroke. Swim one length of the pool with each of these drills: Drill 7—Rowboat, Drill 8—Cymbals, and Drill 14—Stretch and Streamline (beginners and intermediates; or Drill 5—Hands Locked Over Head and Drill 11ffWater-Ski Jump (experienced only). Finish tuning up your muscles with Drill 15, swimming one length each of Build-Up Swims A through D.

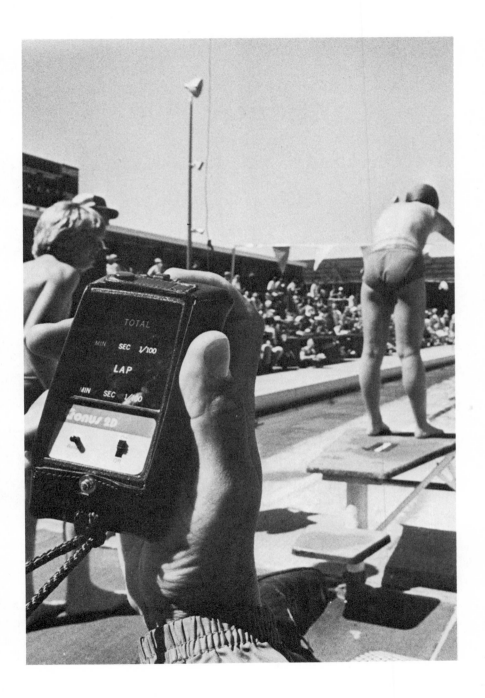

Chapter Five

DRILLS FOR THE BREASTSTROKE

The breaststroke is a much different way of moving through the water than the front or back crawl. In the breaststroke, both your hands will pull and recover in the same pattern at the same time. In your breaststroke kick, or whip kick, both your feet will push, squeeze together, and recover at the same time. Your hands and feet will move in circular patterns. You will swim in a chest-down position and look forward as you lift your head to breathe.

In the breaststroke, as in the front and back crawl, it is important to keep your body as high in the water as possible. By moving your hips gently up and down as you kick, you can keep your feet and legs closer to the surface.

To start your stroke, begin your kick as you begin pulling back with your hands. Lift your head forward for a breath, and bend your knees. Bring your heels up toward your hips just under the surface of the water. Stretch your arms forward as your face goes into the water and you push your feet back to complete the kick. Your hands will pull while you take a breath and recover your legs; your feet will kick and push you forward while your arms recover and your face returns to the water.

It sounds harder than it is. The drills will make it much easier for you. As you practice the drills, your kick will become smooth, continuous, and long. You will begin to feel that your hips and legs are high in the water. Your body will offer less drag.

DRILLS FOR FINDING YOUR OWN STROKE

As you practice these drills for the breaststroke, your body will learn from itself. Be aware of how your arms and legs are working together to push you through the water.

Drill 1—Heels And Hips With Kickboard L,T

Hold a kickboard on the surface of the water in front of you. Keep your face in the water unless you need a breath. From a front float position, arch your back and lift your heels to the surface of the water. Bend your knees and keep your heels at the surface as you bring them up to your hips. As you push back with your feet, bring your hips to the surface by bending and pressing your chest down. Squeeze your legs together, arch your back, and lift your heels at the end of the kick. Keep your heels up as you bend your knees for another kick. Heels up as you squeeze and recover, hips up as you kick back—heels, hips, heels, hips (Fig. 26).

Because the breaststroke kick is back and down, your legs tend to sink. The Heels-and-Hips drills will teach you to bring your legs higher in the water.

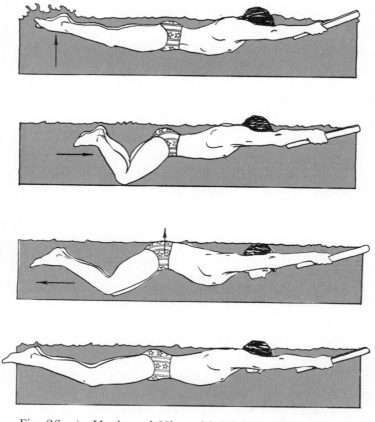

Fig. 26 / Heels and Hips with Kickboard. Drill 1. (a) Arch back and lift heels. (b) Bend Knees. (c) Bring hips to surface of water. (d) Squeeze legs together and arch back.

Drill 2—Heels And Hips Without Kickboard L, T

Practice your kick as you did in Drill 1, but this time do not use a kickboard. Keep your face in the water and your arms stretched out on the water above your head. Push down on the water and lift your head to breathe. How many heels and hips can you do on one breath. Feel the rhythm?

Drill 3—Hand And Heel Touch L, T

Practice your Heels-and-Hips Drill, but this time keep your arms at your sides. Touch your heels with your hands each time you bring them up to kick.

Drill 4—Waiter Whip Kick on Back L, T, S

Float on your back and hold a kickboard with both hands above your chest like a waiter's tray. Practice your kick on your back.

By overloading your kick, you will find the sustaining rhythm that supports you and keeps you moving continuously.

Drill 5—Bronco-Busting Arm Pull L,T

Put your kickboard behind your knees and bend your legs to hold it beneath you. Sit on it with your head above water and ride it like a bucking bronco. You will need to pull hard with your hands to keep your balance and move yourself forward. You should feel your elbows brush against your sides as you bring your hands together. Spear your hands quickly forward to take another pull. Ride the bronco smoothly without bobbing or losing your balance.

Drill 6—Sitting And Floating Scull L, T

Can you scull with your hands to move yourself backward? Hold a kickboard between your legs and float on your back. Hold your arms at your sides. Push the water away from your thighs with the palms of your hands. Then turn your palms toward your thighs and pull in toward your body. Continue to push away and to pull in. Your hands will make a figure 8. If you are moving head-first backward, you are sculling (Fig. 27).

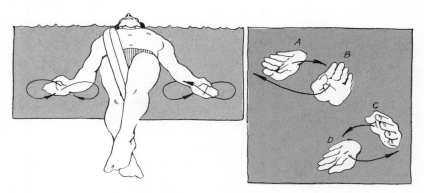

Fig. 27 / Floating Scull. Drill 6. Detail of figure 8 hand movement.

Now float in a sitting position. Scull with your hands, and control the water so that you move backward.

Move again into a back float position, and scull without a kickboard. Keep your body straight, your toes on the surface, and scull for a length of the pool.

Drill 7—Feet-First Float L, T

Hold a kickboard between your knees, and float on your back. Control the water with your hands so that you can move feet-first down the pool on your back.

Drill 8—Bronco-Busting Cymbal Player L, T, S, X

Sit in the water and pull yourself forward as you did in

Drill 5. This time bang your hands together like cymbals before you spear them forward. This will help you spear the water and feel the continuous movement of your hands.

Drill 9—Up-Stretch L, T

Begin in a front float position with your arms stretched above your head. As you bring your heels up to your hips at the surface of the water, still keeping your fingers pointed forward, bring your hands back to touch your forehead. As you push back with your kick, spear your hands forward for a long glide and *stretch* (Fig. 28). Use your Heels-and-Hips kick as in Drill 1. Begin at the end of your kick with your legs straight, your face in the water, and your arms stretched forward in a glide position. Now—*up*—bring your heels up to your hips and touch your forehead with your hands. STRETCH—spear your hands forward and kick. UP—STRETCH—UP—STRETCH!

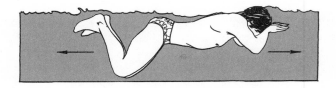

Fig. 28 / Up-Stretch. Drill 9.

Drill 10—Heels And Chin L, T

Swim as in Drill 9, but as you bring your heels up to your hips, lift your head and touch your hands to your chin. Spear the water with your hands as you push with your feet and put your face back into the water (Fig. 29).

Drill 11—Heels, Chin, And Breathe L, T

Swim as in Drill 10, but now as you touch the back of your hands to your chin, take a breath. Blow your breath out while you stretch your arms above your head and kick.

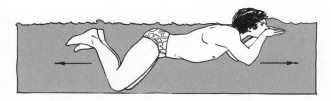

Fig. 29 / Heels and Chin. Drill 10.

DRILLS TO REFINE YOUR STROKE

Drills 1–11 have helped you learn your best natural breaststroke. Is your stroke smooth, synchronized, and continuous? Do you feel pencil-thin so that your body offers almost no resistance to the water? Are your kick and pull timed so that your muscles are always working together? Are you swimming high in the water? Good! Now you are ready to refine and tune up your breaststroke for the greatest speed.

Drill 12—Heels And Hips, Head Up L, T, S, X

Warm up for this drill by practicing your Heels-and-Hips kick with a kickboard as in Drill 1, but this time keep your head above the water.

Now try the Heels-and-Hips kick without a board. Keep your arms stretched out in front of you and your head above the water. You are making your legs work harder, or overloading your stroke. By overloading parts of your stroke, you will perfect your timing.

Drill 13—Waiter Treading Water L, T, S

Stay in the same spot and use your whip kick while you tread water. Hold a kickboard with both hands above your head. You will have to kick fast to keep your arms and head above water. Next, try to kick hard enough to keep your elbows above the water. Keep your tray steady! Try not to bob.

Drill 14—Overlapping Feet L, T

Practice your Heels-and-Hips Drill once again, but overlap your feet as you squeeze them together. This will help you feel the continuous, circular pattern your feet should be making.

Drill 15—Swim Breaststroke L, T

As you lift your heels, pull back on the water with a Bronco-Buster pull. As you pull back, lift your head to breathe. Put your face back into the water and spear your hands forward as you kick. UP—recover legs, pull and breathe. STRETCH—spear hands forward and kick.

Drill 16—Build-Up Swims T, S

Swim the breaststroke, but . . .

A. THINK KICK! Think of throwing the water off your toes as you push your feet back. Then overlap your feet and bend your knees to recover.

B. THINK PULL! Keep feeling your kick, but think of your hands pulling hard.

C. THINK UP-STRETCH! UP—recover your legs, pull hard, and breathe. STRETCH—spear your hands forward and kick hard.

D. THINK SPEED! Build up speed. Kick and pull harder and faster. Swim high and flat in the water.

WARM-UP DRILLS

At the beginning of each practice session and before every swim meet, resensitize your muscles with warm-up drills for the breaststroke. Swim one length of the pool with each of these drills: Drill 2—Heels and Hips Without Kickboard, Drill 5—Bronco-Busting Arm Pull (beginners and intermediates), or Drill 8—Bronco-Busting Cymbal Player (experienced only), and Drill 9—Up-Stretch. Finish tuning up your muscles with Drill 16, swimming one length each of Build-Up Swims A through D.

Chapter Six

DRILLS FOR THE BUTTERFLY

In the butterfly stroke, your body will move in a continuous, rhythmic, up-and-down motion which is similar to the movement that carries a dolphin or porpoise through the water. It might also be compared to the wriggling of a snake or fish except that it goes up and down rather than side to side.

The butterfly kick, or dolphin kick, is much like the flutter kick. However, instead of one foot kicking down while the other kicks up, your feet will move up and down together. Your arms will recover together above the water and pull together beneath the water. You will kick twice as your arms pull: kick once as your hands enter the water, then kick again as your hands finish the push and start to recover.

Look straight ahead and take a breath as your hands pull. Be sure that your head ducks back in the water before your hands go in for another pull (Fig. 30).

Fig. 30 / Butterfly Stroke. (a) Feet kick together. Arms pull together. (b) Hips bend. Pelvis arches. (c) Head looks forward. Arms pull downward. (d) Take a breath. (e) Head ducks back into the water.

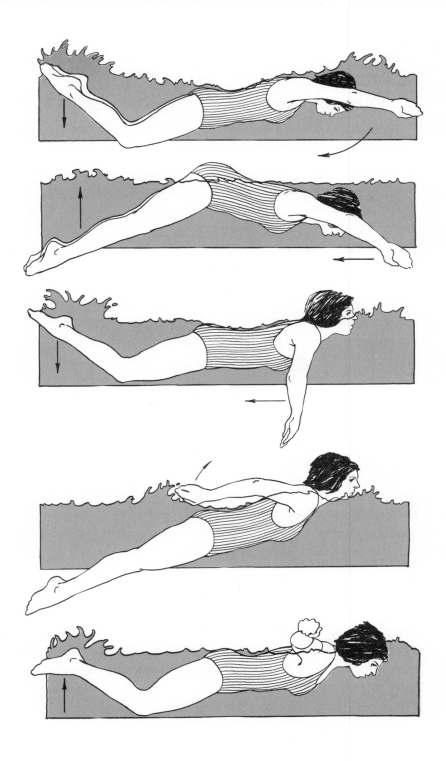

DRILLS FOR FINDING YOUR OWN STROKE

Although the butterfly may be the most difficult stroke to do well, you will find your best natural stroke if you learn from your body as you do these drills. Swim like a dolphin. Feel rhythmic and relaxed as your arms and legs move the water.

Drill 1—Dolphin Swim L, T

Float on your stomach with your arms at your sides. Move through the water like a dolphin or porpoise. Bend at the hips as you kick your feet up and down like a dolphin's tail. As you kick your feet and legs up, your hips will go down. Try using a big kick by bending more at your hips. Then try a smaller kick with less hip bend. Your whole body from your head to your toes should be moving in a flowing pattern like ocean waves.

Drill 2—Back Dolphin Swim L, T

Swim on your back with your arms at your sides. Your hips will move gently up and down as you kick. Flick the water back toward the end of the pool and off the ends of your toes. Your legs and feet move up and down together like a dolphin's tail. Keep your head steady as your body moves.

Drill 3—Snake Wriggle L, T, S, X

Kick on your right side with your right arm extended and pressed against your ear and your left arm at your side. Move through the water by wriggling like a snake. This will develop a strong kick because you must kick harder to stay on your side. Wriggle like a snake on your right side, then on your left (Fig. 31).

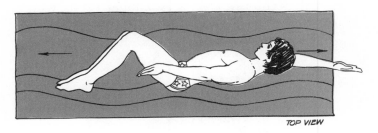

Fig. 31   /   Snake Wriggle. Drill 3.

Drill 4—Dolphin With Kickboard L, T

Hold a kickboard at arm's length in front of you, and kick as in Drill 1. Your shoulders will dip as they did when your arms were at your sides. Your legs and feet are pushing you through the water. Feel that your are kicking back toward the end of the pool rather than just up and down. Try this drill on your front and on your back.

Drill 5—Broken-Wing Recovery L, T

As you swim the butterfly, your shoulders should snap forward like a whip. First try snapping your shoulders while standing on the deck. Put a towel across your shoulder and hold a corner at your chest. Try to jackknife your body so that you can throw the towel up, off your back, and over your shoulder (Fig. 32).

Use the same forward thrust of your shoulders to throw your arms forward in this drill. Pretend your arms are broken wings. Flop them forward by pressing your chest quickly to the bottom of the pool. Let your arms flop wider than you would normally as they enter the water. If you were standing in the center of a clock looking at 12:00, your arms would flop into the water at 10:00 and 2:00 (Fig. 32).

TOP VIEW

Fig. 32 / Broken-Wing Recovery. Drill 5.

Drill 6—Dolphin With Arms Extended L, T, S

Kick as in Drill 4, but without a kickboard. Kick on your stomach with your arms extended in front of you. Then kick on your back with your arms stretched above your head.

Drill 7—Butterfly Scooter L, T

Hold a kickboard beneath your left arm and in front of you on the surface of the water. Pull with your right arm as you kick. Kick twice while your arm makes one circle. Kick as your hand enters the water to begin the pull, and kick again as your hand brushes by your thigh. This will help you feel the timing of your kick and pull (Fig. 33).

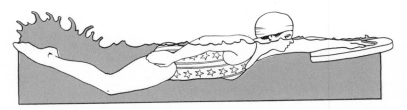

Fig. 33 / Butterfly Scooter. Drill 7. (a) Kick as hand enters water. (b) Kick as hand brushes thigh.

When you have practiced pulling with your right arm, hold the board with your right arm and pull with your left. As in your other strokes, you will get more power if you pull at an even depth beneath the water.

Drill 8—One-Arm Pull Without Kickboard L, T, S

Pull and kick as in Drill 7, but without a kickboard. Pull with your right arm while your left is stretched on the water in front of you. Then stretch out your right arm and pull with your left (Fig. 34).

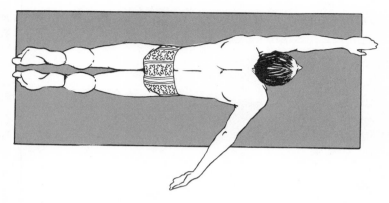

Fig. 34 / One-Arm Pull without Kickboard. Drill 8.

Drill 9—Single to Double Arm Pull L, T

Swim half the length of the pool with one arm extended and the other pulling as in Drill 7. Swim the last half of the pool, pulling with both arms together. Continue the rhythmic bending of your hips as you kick and pull with both arms. You will find the rhythm that you will use in your double arm pull.

Drill 10—Single And Double Arm Pull And Breathe L, T

Swim as in Drill 8, but breathe as soon as you are pulling with both arms. Spear your head straight forward as you begin your pull. Then lift your head, look forward, and take a breath as your hands push toward your thighs.

Drill 11—Hip Popper L, T

Swim with both arms, and kick. As you push your chest to the bottom, think of popping your hips up as if you were standing and using them to open a door. Popping your hips helps you *transfer momentum* from your body to your shoulders and arms.

DRILLS TO REFINE YOUR STROKE

Drills 1–11 have helped you find your natural butterfly stroke. Do you feel supple and loose? Do your arms float out of the water as light as feathers?

When you press your chest down, your arms should feel as if you are stretching for a yawn. Your strong kick just as your arms are about to emerge from the water may make you feel like a porpoise flying out of the sea.

Now use your natural stroke to refine and tune up your butterfly for speed.

Drill 12—Broken-Leg Dolphin Kick L, T, S

Kick on your front with a kickboard held at arm's length ahead of you. Now bend one knee and hold your foot above the water as you kick with the other leg. Kick with your right leg alone, then your left (Fig. 35). Now try the drill without a kickboard. Extend your arms on the water above your head.

Fig. 35 / Broken-Leg Dolphin Kick. Drill 12.

This will sensitize your leg to kick with the proper timing and intensity.

Drill 13—Waiter With Dolphin on Back L, T, S

Kick with a dolphin kick on your back. Hold a kickboard above the surface of the water with both hands. When you first try the drill, you may bend your arms. Then try it with your arms straight so that your body must support the entire weight of your arms and the board. Your legs will have to work harder to keep you high in the water. Hold the board high and kick hard.

Drill 14—Heads-Up Kick L, T, S, X

Practice your dolphin kick with your head out of the water. Practice first with your arms extended in front of you (Fig. 36). Then kick with your hands locked behind your head. This will overload your kick and make you kick faster.

Fig. 36 / Heads-Up Kick. Drill 14.

Drill 15—Two, One, Two L, T

Pull twice with your right arm as you kick, then once with both arms, then twice with your left arm, then once again with both arms—right right, both, left left, both. Continue for the length of the pool, taking your breath on the double arm pull. Feel the timing and rhythm of your stroke?

Drill 16—Heads-Up Butterfly L, T, S

⊙verload your butterfly stroke by holding your head out of the water while you swim with both arms and kick. You will have to kick and pull harder and faster to keep your head on the surface. This will help you develop a sprint stroke.

Drill 17—Periscope Up L, T, S, X

Swim with a double arm pull, but with one leg only. Bend your other leg at the knee so that your foot is above the water. Feel your kick work with your arms to push you through the water? Find the *balance* between your kick and pull that feels right to you (Fig. 37).

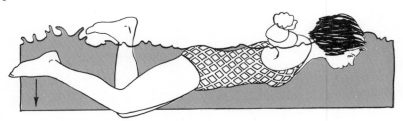

Fig. 37 / Periscope Up. Drill 17.

Drill 18—V In/ V Out L, T

Reach forward above the water to pull with your thumbs leading. Let your hands enter the water positioned as wide or wider apart than your shoulders. Push your palms out as if you were smoothing sand. Then *V in* by pulling your hands toward the center of your body as if you were centering a football between your legs. *V out* by brushing your thighs as you start your recovery. Let your hands bend at your wrists like wings as your arms fly forward for another stroke (Fig. 38).

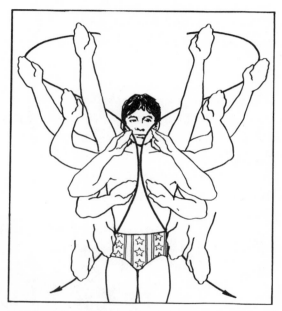

Fig. 38 / V In and V Out. Drill 18.

Drill 19—Build-Up Swims T, S
Swim your whole butterfly stroke, but . . .
A. THINK KICK! Think of your kick pushing you through

the water. Flick the water off your toes as your ankles flop.

B. THINK PULL! Keep kicking, but think of your arms pulling hard as you V IN and pushing hard as you V OUT and *follow through.*

C. THINK KICK AND PULL! Think of your kick pushing, your arms pulling and pushing.

D. THINK SPEED! Build up speed. Kick and pull harder and faster. Swim high in the water with a shallow pull.

WARM-UP DRILLS

At the beginning of each practice and before every swim meet, resensitize your muscles with these warm-up drills for the butterfly. Swim a length of the pool with each drill: Drill 6—Dolphin with Arms Extended, Drill 7—Butterfly Scooter, Drill 8—One-Arm Pull without Kickboard, and Drill 16—Heads-Up Butterfly. Finish tuning up your muscles with Drill 19, swimming one length each of Build-Up Swims A through D.

Chapter Seven

STARTS

Places in swimming competition are often separated by mere fractions of a second, so your start is extremely important. A long, flat dive for distance will give you the greatest speed at the start of your race. As you spear and penetrate the surface, your arms should be stretched forward and over your ears. The last thing you will feel is the drive of your pointed toes as they enter the water.

As you practice your starting dives, you will become more comfortable with the feeling of landing nearly flat in the water. Do at least two or three starts at the end of every practice session.

FORWARD STARTS

The starts for the three forward strokes—freestyle, breaststroke, and butterfly—are the same for the first four phases of action. There *is* a difference in flight, entry, and pull-out, however.

Action I—Take Starting Position

As the race is about to begin, take a position standing upright on the block. Your feet should be about a shoulder-width apart with all your toes curled over the forward edge of the block. This will make your feet slightly pigeon-toed (Fig. 39a).

Action II—Get Ready For Start

At the signal "take your marks" from the starter, bend over as if to touch your toes and bend slightly at your knees. Shift your weight forward to the balls of your feet, but keep your heels in light contact with the block (Fig. 39b).

The starter will not shoot the gun until all swimmers are

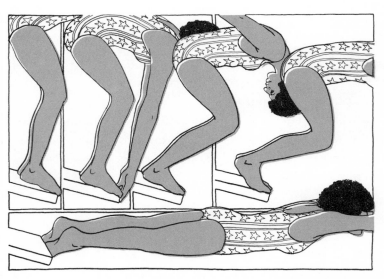

Fig. 39 / Forward Starts. (a) Action I. Take Starting Position. (b) Action II. Get Ready for Start. (c and d) Action III. Knee Drop. (e) Action IV. Push and Extend.

motionless. Don't move but stay loose. Don't freeze into position. Look at your feet.

Action III—Knee Drop

At the sound of the gun signaling the start, drop your knees forward and down toward the water (Fig. 39c and d).

Action IV—Push And Extend

Push with your feet and extend your legs so that you push out parallel to the surface of the water. Throw your arms forward hard (Fig. 39e).

FREESTYLE START

Action V—Flight

The flight phase for the freestyle start should be longer and flatter than the start for the breaststroke or butterfly. Your head should be up, and you should be looking at your fingertips. Your body should be straight and your toes pointed.

Action VI—Entry

Your hands will enter the water first, followed by your head, your torso, and your legs. You should hit the water nearly flat, as if you were skipping a stone. Drop your head between your arms just before you hit the surface. Begin a very shallow, toe-pointed kick as soon as you enter the water (Fig. 40).

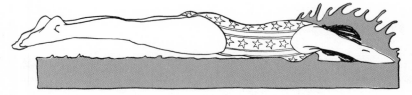

Fig. 40 / Entry. Action VI.

Action VII—Pull-Out

The pull-out is the final action in the freestyle start. It combines arm-and-leg motion with the dive to pull the swimmer into position for the first stroke on the surface (Fig. 41).

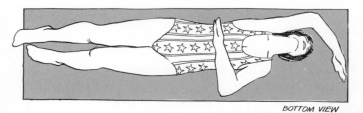

Fig. 41 / Pull-Out. Action VII.

Although in the freestyle there is an alternate arm action, in the pull-out one arm follows the other very closely to continue the speed of the dive. The arms pull shallow and long beneath the body. The recovery of the first two strokes should exaggerate the forward reach of the arms.

DRILLS FOR FREESTYLE START

Drill 1—Sitting Start

Sit on the edge of the pool with your feet in the gutter. Lean forward, maintaining your balance, until the line from your ankle to your knee is parallel to the water. Continue to move, but now extend your legs behind you and push. Fire your body like a cannon about 6 inches above the surface of the water. Keep your head up as you hit the water. The line from your ankle to your knee as you push will point the direction in which you will dive (Fig. 42).

Fig. 42 / Sitting Start. Drill 1. (a) Boat launch: Correct way to enter water. (b) Belly flop: Incorrect way to enter water.

If you do this correctly, your body will hit the water like a boat being launched. Be sure that you are not too high and that you do not drop flat onto the water in a "belly flop."

Drill 2—Head Drop

Push from a sitting start as in Drill 1, but this time drop your head between your arms just before you enter the water.

Drill 3—Dive And Reach

Dive again from a sitting start. Have a partner hold a pole just above the surface of the water twice as far away from you as you are tall. Stretch your body and reach toward the pole as you dive. Try to touch it just before you enter the water.

Drill 4—Dive And Stretch

Stand by the pool with all your toes over the edge. Hold your hands together behind your back. Drop your knees

Fig. 43   /   Dive and Stretch. Drill 4.

and begin to extend your legs with your hands still behind you. Throw your arms forward just as you fully extend your legs (Fig. 43).

This drill will help you feel the point at which the thrust of your arms should be added to the push of your legs.

DRILLS FOR THE FREESTYLE GRAB START

The grab start is recognized as the fastest forward start. Not only your feet, but also your hands, are used to push off the block. Because your center of gravity is lower, your flight is closer to the water and your entry will be faster. In addition, holding onto the block reduces the chance of mistakes in the start.

The next three drills will help you learn the freestyle grab start.

Drill 5—Drop And Push

Move two starting blocks on either side of you about 6 inches outside of each shoulder. If you do not have starting blocks handy, two other swimmers—one on either side of you—can kneel on their outside knees. Their legs closest to you should be bent, with their toes at the edge of the pool.

Stand by the pool with all your toes curled over the edge. The palms of your hands should be back and against the blocks or the knees of the other swimmers (Fig. 44).

Drop your knees toward the water. As soon as your lower legs are parallel to the surface, push with your hands off the blocks or knees beside you. Throw your arms straight ahead as you extend your legs.

When you are in flight, your head should be lifted and you

Fig. 44 / Drop and Push. Drill 5.

should be looking forward at your fingertips. Your body should be straight and your toes pointed. Drop your head between your arms just before you enter the water.

This drill will help you learn timing and the importance of using your hands in a grab start.

Drill 6—Drop-And-Push On Blocks

Stand on a starting block with your toes curled over the edge. Two other swimmers should stand on either side of you. They should lift the foot closest to you to the block so that their knees are beside yours.

Put the palms of your hands on the knee to your right and the knee to your left. Drop your knees toward the water. Push off with your hands as you extend your legs. You will feel the timing of pushing and extending that you will use in the grab start.

The greater height of the block will give you a greater distance over the water. You will keep your head up longer than you did in Drill 5.

Drill 7—Grab Start

Grab the front of the starting block with your hands just outside your feet. Pull yourself down over the block. Look at your feet and pull lightly on the block with your hands. At the same time, push and try to extend your legs. Your arms and legs will be working together and will make you feel like a compressed spring. Your muscles will be tense, but not frozen, ready for the start (Fig. 45a).

At the sound of the gun, stay in your tensed position, but start rolling forward until your body weight is no longer over your feet. Then, still looking at your feet, drop your knees and drive them forward and down over the water (Fig. 45b).

When your lower legs are parallel to the water, push off the block, throw your arms forward and lift your head to look at your fingertips. Drop your head between your arms just before you enter the water (Fig. 45c).

Drill 8—Pull-Out For Freestyle

Begin this drill with the Grab Start as in Drill 7. Drop your

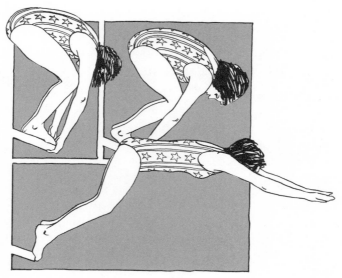

Fig. 45 / Grab Start. Drill 7. (a) Grab starting block. (b) Roll forward. (c) Push off from block.

head between your arms just before you enter the water and begin a shallow, toe-pointed kick.

As soon as you are in the water, pull with your right arm and then, immediately, with your left. It will be almost like a double arm pull. Your elbows should be bent so that your hands nearly touch your body as they pull and push back toward your feet. This is an exaggerated, shallow, long stroke. Pull extra long and reach extra far forward to recover.

BREASTSTROKE AND BUTTERFLY STARTS

Actions I–IV are the same for the breaststroke and butterfly as for the freestyle and were discussed as forward starts at the beginning of this chapter. Review the first four phases of the start before continuing with Action V.

Action V—Flight

In the flight phase of the breaststroke and butterfly starts, as in the freestyle, your head should be up and facing your fingertips, but your back must arch to help lift your legs. Lift your heels so that they are higher than your head. Pretend there is a rope or pole floating on the water some distance away. As you dive over it, arch your back and bend your

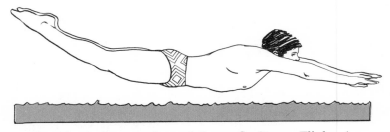

Fig. 46 / Breastroke and Butterfly Starts. Flight. Action V.

knees to keep your feet from hitting it. You will tuck your head between your arms sooner than you did in the freestyle start to achieve a deeper entry (Fig. 46).

Action VI—Entry

Enter the water as if you were diving into a hole. Straighten your legs as soon as they are beneath the surface. There should be very little splash from your dive and no splash from the straightening of your legs (Fig. 47).

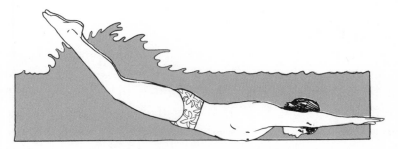

Fig. 47 / Breastroke and Butterfly Starts. Entry. Action VI.

Action VII—Pull-Out

Since arms and legs are used differently in the breaststroke and the butterfly, the pull-out action that brings the swimmer into position for the first surface stroke will be different in each.

Drills 2 and 3 will teach you the fastest and easiest pull-out for the breaststroke and butterfly.

DRILLS FOR BREASTSTROKE AND BUTTERFLY STARTS

Drill 1—Lane Line Dive

Have two swimmers hold a rope on the surface of the water so it is one foot closer to you than your height. Dive over it at that distance. Then have them move it gradually away from you until it is as far away as you are tall.

Imagine a hole on the other side of the lane line. Dive into the hole with as little splash as possible. As you dive, arch your back and lift your heels (see Fig. 47). Lift your feet as if you were going to kick the back of your head.

Press your arms hard against your ears as you spear the water, and straighten your legs again quickly. Point your toes as you enter the water, and glide.

Drill 2—Pull-Out For Breaststroke

Spear the water as you dive into a hole, and glide. Turn your hands so that your palms are together. Then, keeping your palms together, bend your elbows and bring your hands down until they are beneath your nose.

When your hands are beneath your face, turn your palms toward your feet, catch the water and throw it straight toward your toes. Snap your wrists as you throw the water off your fingertips. As you snap your wrists, turn your hands so that the palms are on your thighs (Fig. 48).

Recover your hands together close to your body. As your hands move under your chin, recover your legs for a kick. Kick, look up, and reach for the surface. Take a breath on your first surface stroke.

Drill 3—Pull-Out For Butterfly

Kick one dolphin kick as soon as you are in the water. Turn your hands so that your palms are together. Then bend your elbows and bring your hands down together until they are beneath your nose. Let your hands come apart beneath your face to pull your body forward. Kick again as

Fig. 48 / Pull-Out for Breaststroke. Drill 2. (a) Glide with palms together. (b) Bend elbows, bring hands beneath nose. (c) Turn palms toward feet. (d) Snap wrists, turn hands so palms touch thighs.

you V out and push back and away from your hips. As you start to V out, lift your head and take a breath.

Some swimmers prefer to take one or two strokes before taking a breath. This permits a more horizontal position.

BACKSTROKE START

Action I—Take Starting Position

Stand on the bottom of the pool facing the starting block. When the race is about to start, shake the excess water off your hands. Then grasp the part of the starting block that is intended for the backstroke start. Place your feet on the pool gutter. If there is no gutter, place them just under the surface of the water. If it is a long-course race (50 meters or yards), international instead of American rules must be followed. This means you must start with your toes beneath the water rather than on the gutter. Now, bend your knees and tuck your hips close to your heels (Fig. 49a).

Action II—Get Ready For Start

At the signal "take your marks" from the starter, bend your arms and pull yourself into a relaxed tuck position. hips should remain close to your heels. Your chin your chest and your forehead close to your

And Extend

uickly pull your body up as high push yourself backward with Clear the surface of the

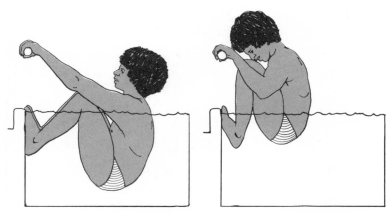

Fig. 49 / Backstroke Start. (a) Action I. Take Starting Position. (b) Action II. Get Ready for Start.

water as if you were diving backward over a kickboard. As you extend your legs, look back and circle your hands around your head. Keep them just above the surface of the water with your palms up until they are stretched above your head (Fig. 49c).

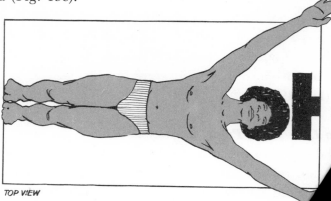

TOP VIEW

(c) Action III. Tuck, Push, and Extend.

Action IV— Flight

In flight, your body will be sightly arched. Your head will be looking back at your fingertips. Your legs should be straight and your toes pointed (Fig. 49d).

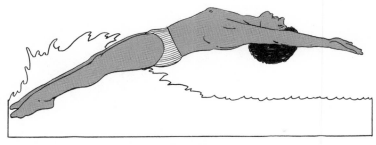

(d) Action IV. Flight.

Action V—Entry

You should remain in your arched position so that your hands enter the water first. Keep your arms pressed tightly against your ears (Fig. 49e).

Start your kick as soon as you are in the water. It should be fast and much shallower (only about 6 inches deep) than the kick you will use later with your backstroke.

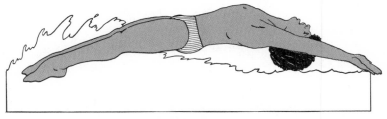

(e) Action V. Entry.

Action VI—Pull-Out

Continue your shallow kick for two arm strokes. Pull with your right arm, and brush your thigh with your hand as it goes past. Pull with your left arm immediately following your right. Brush your thigh with your left hand. Your arms will pull almost at the same time. Recover your hands extra long on your first two strokes by stretching your arms and body as though reaching (Fig. 49f).

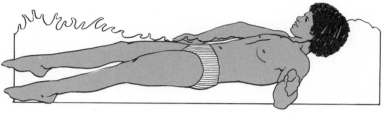

(f) Action VI. Pull-Out.

DRILLS FOR BACKSTROKE START

Drill 1—Boat Launching

Push out from the backstroke starting position and extend your legs. Leave your hands on your thighs and keep your chin tucked down on your chest. How far can you glide with one push? The straighter you can make your body, the farther you will be able to glide.

Drill 2—Drop, Feather, And Push

Hold the gutter or side of the pool with both hands. Your feet should be on the wall and close to the surface.

Let go of the wall with your hands and drop under water. Lie back so that your body is parallel to the surface. Feather your hands, as you would feather the oars of a boat, by turning your palms up. Let your elbows bend as your hands make a circle around your head.

As your arms straighten and your hands come together above your head, push off with your feet and glide (Fig. 50).

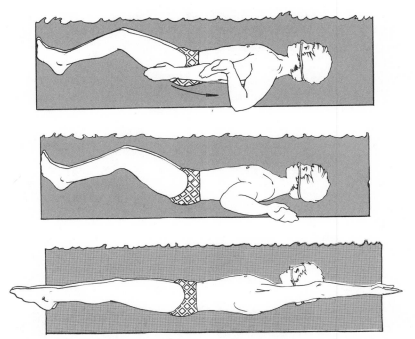

Fig. 50 / Drop, Feather, and Push. Drill 2. (a) Feather hands, turn palms up. (b) Bend elbows, hands circle around to head. (c) Arms straighten, hands come together above head. Note: Nose plugs keep water out of sinus passages.

Drill 3—Dive Over Kickboard

Have a partner hold a kickboard about 8–10 inches behind your back while you hold the block in a starting position. Push off and dive backward over the kickboard. Your hips should clear the board.

Your partner can duck under the water before you start your dive to avoid your arms, or you can hold your arms at your sides as you dive.

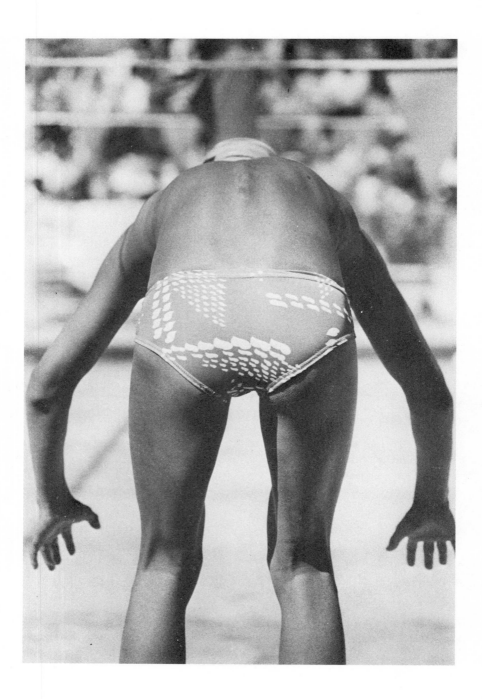

Chapter Eight

TURNS

A good turn can increase your speed and help you make up time in a race. Your attitude toward turns in practice will become important in competition. Don't rest on your turns! A champion swimmer "attacks" the wall. He or she swims hard into the wall, makes a fast, smooth turn, and pushes off quickly and forcefully.

You will be able to make your turns quickly and easily if your body is in a tight ball during the turn and is fired into and away from the wall in a straight line. The tighter the ball your body can make the faster it will turn.

It is also important to keep your feet and hands close to the surface of the water, following a straight line to your target. The lane marker on the bottom of the pool will mark the line your body should follow to your target on the wall and back to the opposite wall.

Imagine a line directly above the lane marker on the bottom of the pool and parallel to and near the surface of the water. Try to keep your feet and hands as close to this line as you can while making your turns.

FREESTYLE TURN

Action I—Preparation

Every competitive pool has a target mark for turns at the end of each lane. It is usually a black square, but it may be a cross. The target mark is approximately the spot where your feet should hit the wall to push off.

Continue to kick as you look at the target. Experienced swimmers will sense their feet on the wall as soon as they see the mark (Fig. 51a).

Action II—Pike And Roll

Bend at your waist as if you were pushing your chest to your thighs. Keep your legs straight. Hold one arm straight at your side, pointing at your feet. Bend the arm that's in

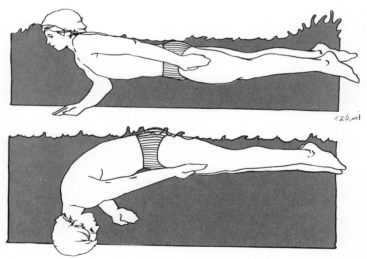

Fig. 51 / Freestyle Turn. (a) Action I. Preparation. (b) Action II. Pike and Roll.

front of you and move it under your chin and under your body parallel to the surface of the water (Fig. 51b).

Action III—Heel, Kick, And Extend

Let your hand continue to move in the direction you will be swimming.

Bend your legs as if to kick yourself in the seat. Now keep your hands and feet on a straight line above the lane marker and let your legs flip over like a pinwheel. Extend your legs toward the wall and push your feet against the target (Fig. 51c).

As your feet hit the wall, they should be separated and parallel. Both hands should be pointing in the new direction.

(c) Action III. Heel, Kick, and Extend.

Action IV—Extend And Push

Continue to extend as your feet hit the wall. Push off hard with your toes as your legs straighten. Both arms will be stretching above your head and covering your ears (Fig. 51d).

Action V—Pull-Out

The pull-out used with the freestyle turn is exactly the same as that used with the start. The pull is long and shallow, with one arm followed closely by the other (Fig. 51e).

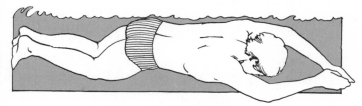

(d) Action IV. Extend and Push.

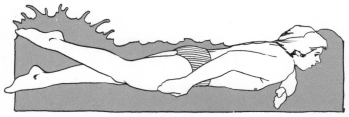

(e) Action V. Pull-Out.

DRILLS FOR FREESTYLE TURN

Drill 1—Left Hand, Right Hand Kickboard

Kick toward the wall, holding a kickboard with both hands. About 5 feet before you reach the wall, bring your kickboard back across the surface of the water with your left hand. Your palm should be down on top of the board.

When your board is next to your left thigh, pull your right hand beneath you in a straight line. As your hand passes beneath your chin, pike as in Action II. Then lift your heels and kick them back to the wall as in Action III. Return your right hand to the board as you kick and extend (Fig. 52).

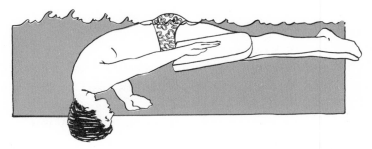

Fig. 52 / Left Hand, Right Hand Kickboard. Drill 1.

Whenever you practice kicking in training, you should make all your turns this way.

Drill 2—Kickboard Kick-Out

Have a partner hold a kickboard against the wall over your target. The board will make a softer cushion for your feet. See how hard you can kick against the kickboard. This will make you more confident about kicking hard into the wall (Fig. 53).

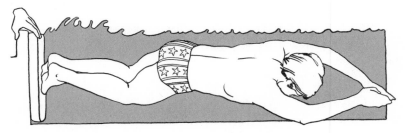

Fig. 53 / Kickboard Kick-Out. Drill 2.

BACKSTROKE TURN

Action I—Preparation

On the last two pulls before you reach the wall, you should recover your arms high and continue to kick to keep your body stretched and flat in the water.

Drop your head back and look under the water at the wall. Find the target spot for your feet to push against.

Action II—Knee Draw And Pivot

Touch the wall with one hand and leave the other arm at your side (Fig. 54a).

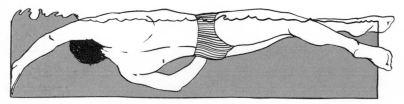

Fig. 54 / Backstroke Turn. (a, b, and c) Action II. Knee Draw and Pivot.

Bend your knees and draw them up toward your nose by bending at the waist. As you draw up your knees, keep your feet at or below the surface of the water so that they are moving in a straight line. Keep your hips high in the water by bringing your knees up and over the surface (Fig. 54b). Don't sit!

When your knees are close to your nose, throw them over your shoulder toward the hand that is on the wall. Your body will pivot if you lean away from the wall as your knees go toward it (Fig. 54c).

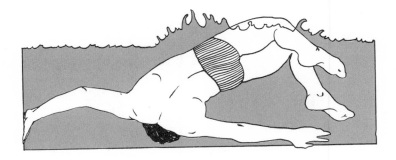

As you pivot, pull your hand off the wall and bring it close to your body. Return it in a straight line to the other hand, which has stayed in a position pointing in the new direction.

Action III—Extend, Push, And Stretch

Your arms should come together and extend above your head at the same time your legs extend. The stretch of your arms and the final push off the wall with your toes should be simultaneous (Fig. 54d).

(d) Action III. Extend, Push, and Stretch.

Action IV—Pull-Out

The pull-out used with the backstroke turn is exactly the same as that used with the start. Begin your fast, shallow kick, then pull with one arm and, quickly, the other. The arms will pull at nearly the same time (Fig. 54e).

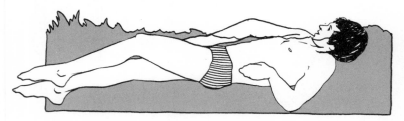

(e) Action IV. Pull-Out.

DRILLS FOR BACKSTROKE TURN

Drill 1—Drop, Feather, And Push

Repeat Drill 2 for the backstroke start to practice pushing off from your turn. Hum through your nose when your head is beneath the surface to keep water out of your nose.

Drill 2—Soap-Slide Drill

Cover a slippery deck or a piece of plastic with soap suds. Lie on your back on this surface with your turning hand on the wall. Your body should be wet enough to slide easily. Flip your knees up and over your shoulder toward your hand. Pivot and push out with your feet.

Drill 3—Flipper

Kick on your back with your right hand above your head as you move toward the wall. Touch the wall and start to bring your knees up. Your partner should lift and flip your knees to help you as you bring them up and over your shoulder. This will keep your hips high in the water and add to the force of your legs as you pivot (Fig. 55).

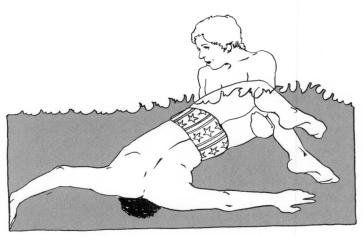

Fig. 55 / Flipper. Drill 3.

Drill 4—Straight Line Checker

Hold a kickboard with your trailing arm as you flip. The board should stay pointing toward the new direction you will be swimming.

Hold one end of the board and have your partner hold the opposite end. He or she should hold the board lightly at first to keep it straight, but should let go as your feet go toward the wall. The board will turn over as your hand and body pivot. Bring the hand that was on the wall back to the board and push off gently on the surface (Fig. 56).

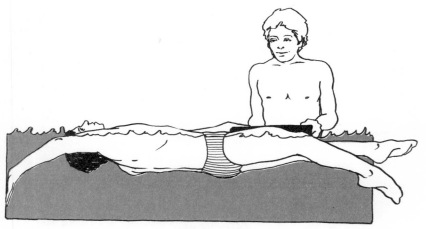

Fig. 56 / Straight Line Checker. Drill 4.

BREASTSTROKE AND BUTTERFLY TURNS

The turns for the breaststroke and butterfly are alike in every phase of action except the last, the pull-out.

Action I—Preparation

As you swim into the wall, keep your body long and your hips near the surface. Your head should be up and your eyes should be just below the surface, looking at the spot where you'll grab the wall. Think of the target on the wall where you'll put your feet to push off (Fig. 57a).

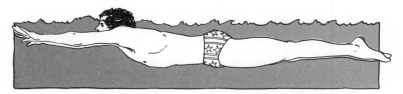

Fig. 57 / Breaststroke and Butterfly Turns. (a) Action I. Preparation.

Action II—Touch And Draw

Grab the wall with both hands and draw up your knees. Your feet should be moving toward your hips in a straight line just under the surface of the water (Fig. 57b).

(b) Action II. Touch and Draw.

Action III—Tuck And Pivot

Your feet will continue to go under your body as you tuck and prepare to pivot. Pull your knees up to the wall and pivot and turn your hips toward the wall.

Your hands will come off the wall together just as your body pivots. Your hands and knees will pass beneath your body as they exchange positions. Keep your hands close to your body and moving in a straight line in the direction you will be swimming (Fig. 57c and d).

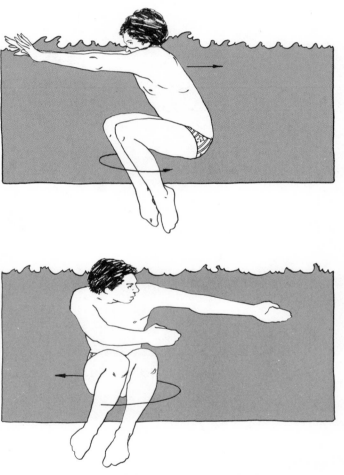

(c and d) Action III. Tuck and Pivot.

As you pivot, keep your shoulders flat and just under the surface of the water. Your hips should also remain close to the surface throughout the turn.

Action IV—Extend, Push, And Reach

After your hands have passed your knees, extend your feet toward the wall. Make contact and continue to extend. Push out with your toes at the same time you reach forward with your arms (Fig. 57e).

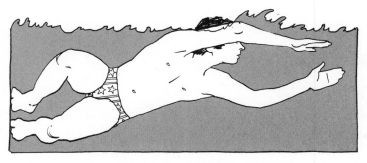

(e) Action IV. Extend, Push, and Reach.

Action V—Pull-Out

The pull-out for the breaststroke and the pull-out for the butterfly are the same as those previously described for each stroke. Practice the pull-outs for your turns by reviewing Drills 2 and 3 for the breaststroke and butterfly starts.

DRILLS FOR BREASTSTROKE AND BUTTERFLY TURNS

Drill 1—Pivot In Place, Head Above Water

Put both hands on the gutter or wall. Flutter kick gently to keep your feet on the surface. Let go with your left hand, but continue to hold with your right.

Tuck your knees and turn them in a *J*. Bend your left elbow and pull it back hard as you pull your hand in a straight line beneath you. Your hand will pass your knees as you pivot and throw your hips toward the wall.

Place your feet on the wall with your toes pointing toward the bottom of the pool. Your shoulders should be flat on the surface. Your left hand should be pointing in the direction you will be swimming (Fig. 58).

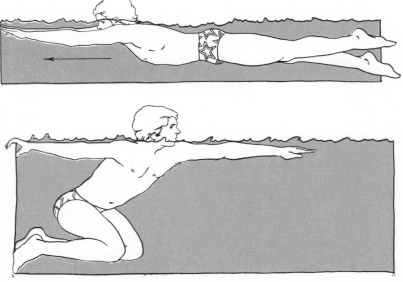

Fig. 58 / Pivot in Place, Head above Water. Drill 1. (a) Begin with both hands on gutter, feet flutter kicking. (b) End with feet on wall, shoulders level at surface, and left hand pointing in direction you will be going.

Drill 2—Pivot In Place, Face In Water

Hold on to the side of the pool with both hands and pivot in place as in Drill 1, but this time keep your face in the water. This will help you keep your hips near the surface.

Drill 3—Tightening The Pivot

Pivot in place with your face in the water as in Drill 2, but try to bring your feet higher on the wall each time you turn.

Drill 4—Tear And Reach

Hold on to the wall with both hands. Your left hand should be on top of your right. Start with your legs extended behind you, then tuck and pivot. As you pivot, tear your right hand off the wall with your left. Reach out with both hands

Fig. 59 / Tear and Reach. Drill 4. (a) Right hand grips wall, left hand grips right hand.

together in the direction you will be swimming. Push off the wall with your toes, and glide as you reach (Fig. 59).

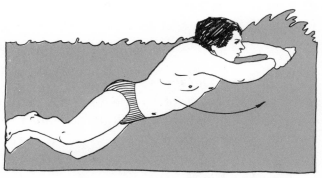

(b) During pivot, left hand tears right hand away from wall.

Chapter Nine
WATER TRAINING

There are two important goals you can achieve through water training. One is to learn and refine your swimming skills. The other is to improve your heart action and blood circulation so that you will become physically fit and able to swim longer distances with greater speed for less effort.

TUNE-UP DRILLS

Your drills have helped you learn the strokes that take the fullest advantage of your natural abilities. The drills should still be used at the beginning of training for each stroke. They will reinforce the skills you have learned and insure that your coordination and timing are in a "tuned-up" condition to take the fullest advantage of your fitness training.

The drills will not only help you continue to use your own natural abilities, but they will let you take advantage of the changes that take place in your own body. As you grow in strength, endurance, and ability, they will help you change and improve. Each new stroke or skill you learn will improve those you have already learned. The more you understand your own movements in the water, the more efficient a swimmer you will become.

In the beginning of your training, or preseason before swim meets begin, you should spend your entire workout on the drills to learn or review your strokes and begin your fitness training. As the season progresses, you will continue the drills as a review or tune-up, but you will spend more and more time on fitness training, using whole strokes, kicking, or pulling. Even during the championship season, it is important to spend at least 25 percent of your time refining skills, coordination, and timing to the highest possible level with drills.

INTERVAL TRAINING

Interval training involves repeating a set distance with a set rest period between each swim. You may, for example, swim a 2,000-meter or yard distance at intervals of 40 repeat swims times 50 meters or yards. If you are training in a 25-meter or yard pool, this would mean.that you would swim 2 lengths of the pool 40 times. Or you may swim the same 2,000 at 20 repeat swims times 100 (4 lengths), or 10 repeat swims times 200 (8 lengths). The rest periods will vary, but they should average about 15 seconds. Kick alone, pull alone, or the complete stroke may be used along with the drills in interval training.

Broken swims are another form of interval training. A 2,000-meter swim may consist of 10 "broken" 200-yard swims. This means each 200 may be broken down into shorter swims—4 times 50, 2 times 100, or 100, 50, and 50.

Swimmers try to swim each part of a broken swim faster than the one before. For instance, 4 times 50 meters might be swum in 31 seconds, 30, 29, and 28.

At the beginning of the season you will build your strength and endurance with interval training at a comfortable speed. From 60 to 70 percent of your best effort is the pace you should set for yourself at first.

To find the time at which you should swim your training interval, divide your best time in seconds by the percentage of effort. If, for instance, you want to swim 200 yards of freestyle at 70 percent of your best effort, and your best time is 2 minutes, 30 seconds, first convert your time to seconds (150). Divide 150 seconds by 70 percent or .70. This will give you 214 as the nearest number of seconds. Divide by 60 to convert back to minutes, and you will have 3 minutes, 34 seconds. You will then know that you should swim your training interval at about 3:34 if you are giving 70 percent of your best effort.

Record your percentage of effort times for each stroke and distance on the PERCENTAGE OF EFFORT chart. Use pencil so that you may easily change it as your best times improve. You can find your percentage times by using this formula:

$$\frac{\text{TIME FOR SWIMMING}}{\text{TRAINING INTERVAL}} = \frac{\text{YOUR BEST TIME}}{\text{PERCENTAGE OF EFFORT}}$$

As the season progresses, your physical fitness will improve. The distances you swim will become longer, and the rest periods will be shorter. You will swim harder, gradually increasing your effort to 80 or 90 percent.

At the end, or championship, part of the season your distances may once again be somewhat shorter and the rest periods between swims may be longer. You can reach your peak of performance at this time by combining the physical fitness you have achieved with the stroke techniques you have learned. Your percentage of effort in this part of your training will rise to 90 percent or more.

PERCENTAGE OF EFFORT
BASED ON YOUR BEST TIMES FOR _____
date

USE THIS FORMULA: $\dfrac{\text{TIME FOR SWIMMING}}{\text{TRAINING INTERVAL}} = \dfrac{\text{YOUR BEST TIME}}{\text{PERCENTAGE OF EFFORT}}$

STROKE	DISTANCE	BEST TIME	60%	70%	80%	90%
FREESTYLE	25 _____ yards or meters					
	50 _____					
	100 _____					
	150 _____					
	200 _____					
BACKSTROKE	25 _____					
	50 _____					
	100 _____					
	150 _____					
	200 _____					
BREASTSTROKE	25 _____					
	50 _____					
	100 _____					
	150 _____					
	200 _____					
BUTTERFLY	25 _____					
	50 _____					
	100 _____					
	150 _____					
	200 _____					

GUIDE FOR WATER TRAINING

Use the figures in the GUIDE FOR WATER TRAINING chart to help you plan your own training program. In the first column, fill in the number of days you will spend in preseason, early competitive, late competitive, and championship training.

Divide the length of your workout by the suggested percentage of time spent on drills or on kicking, pulling, or whole strokes. Enter these times in the second column.

In the third column, write the number of yards or meters you will swim at each distance in your interval training during an average daily workout.

The fourth column suggests the rest between intervals, with more rest in preseason (due to lack of conditioning) and in championship season (to permit higher percentage effort swims). The fifth and sixth columns establish intensity of training, while the seventh and eighth columns describe objectives and outcomes of the use of drills in training.

GUIDE FOR WATER TRAINING

Part of the season / Total length of your season	Percentage of time spent on: drills-whole strokes, kick, or pull	Interval training Distances in meters or yards / Percentage of time spent on each in meters or yards for av. daily workout	Rest between intervals	Quality or percentage of effort	Degree of exertion	Major objectives	Desired outcome
Preseason / days ___	100% - 0 / ___ minutes per workout	25s - 50s - 100s / 25% - 50% - 25% / ___ meters or yards per average workout	5–20 seconds	60% to 70%	Comfortable	To learn or review skills	Progress from unskilled to knowledge of skill
Early competitive / days ___	75% - 25% / ___ minutes per workout	50s - 100s - 150s / 25% - 50% - 25% / ___ meters or yards per average workout	5–10 seconds	70% to 80%	Pushing	Learning and overload for increased fitness	Progress from knowledge of skill to skilled
Later competitive / days ___	50% - 50% / ___ minutes per workout	100s - 150s - 200s / 25% - 50% - 25% / ___ meters or yards per average workout	5–10 seconds	70% to 90%	Pushing to high stress	Overload for increased fitness and pace	Progress from skilled to refinement of skill
Championship / days ___	25% - 75% / ___ minutes per workout	50s - 100s - 200s / 25% - 50% - 25% / ___ meters or yards per average workout	5–30 seconds	60% to 90% or more	Comfortable to high stress	Tune up, refinement, and speed	Progress from refinement of skill to peak of performance

Fill in the blanks according to your training schedule.

DISTANCE TRAINING GRAPH

One way of showing improvement as the season progresses is by increasing the distances you swim in workouts. You can record the average distance you swim each week on the graph for distance training. The line on the graph will tell you how much you are improving.

Keep a record of the number of yards you swim at each workout. These yards may be in drills, kicking, pulling, or whole strokes. At the end of the week, divide the total number of yards by the number of workouts to get your average distance for the week. Extra days in the month should be added to the closest week and divided by the total number of workouts for that period of time.

Extra copies of this graph may be used to record the distance of training for each of the four strokes and for distance of kick alone, pull alone, and drills.

DISTANCE TRAINING GRAPH

AVERAGE
DAILY
YARDS PER WEEK

8,000
7,500
7,000
6,500
6,000
5,500
5,000
4,500
4,000
3,500
3,000
2,500
2,000
1,500
1,000

DATE	1 2 3 4 WEEK OF month	1 2 3 4 WEEK OF month	1 2 3 4 WEEK OF month	1 2 3 4 WEEK OF month	1 2 3 4 WEEK OF month	1 2 3 4 WEEK OF month	1 2 3 4 WEEK OF month	1 2 3 4 WEEK OF month

QUALITY OF TRAINING GRAPH

Your improvement may also be measured by the quality of your training. You should be swimming with a higher percentage of effort as the season progresses.

Keep a record of the number of times in each workout you swim the prescribed distance at 60 percent of your best effort or better. How many times at 70 percent or better? At 80 percent? At 90 percent? At the end of each week divide these

TIMES PERCENTAGE OF EFFORT IS EQUALED OR BETTERED

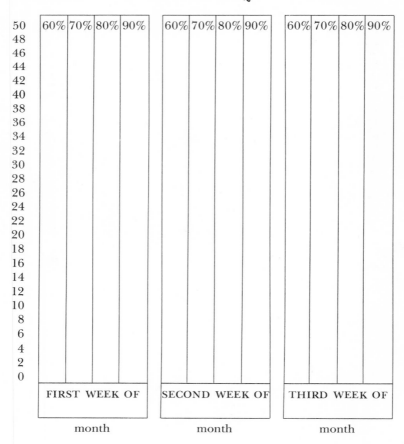

numbers by the number of workouts to find your average. Fill in the number of times you equaled or bettered each percentage of effort on the thermometer graph. Are you getting hotter? An increase in the number of your high percentage efforts will show improvement in the quality of your training.

You may find it useful to make copies of this graph to record your quality of training for each of the four strokes.

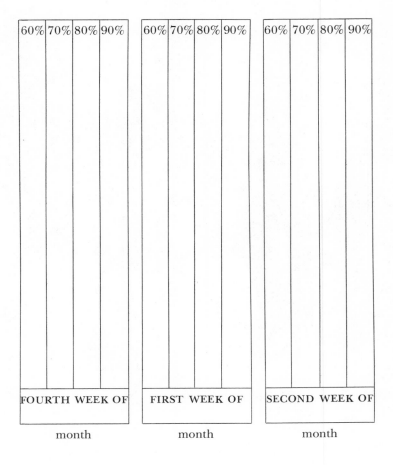

Chapter Ten
DRY LAND TRAINING

There are some parts of a training program that should be carried out on land. Running is an excellent way to improve your heart and lung action and is a good substitute for water training when pool time is limited. Strength, muscular endurance, and flexibility can best be increased with dry land exercises. The following drills can be done with a team or at home with a partner.

In many of your dry land training drills, you must hold or lift a heavy object. A set of barbells would be a wise investment, since they are easy to handle and their weight can be regulated. Although we will refer to barbells in the drills, other heavy objects, such as a stack of books, a chair, or a large shovel may be substituted.

DRILLS FOR ENDURANCE

In the early part of the season, developing endurance is more important than increasing strength. The best way to improve your endurance is to repeat an exercise as many times as possible in a set period of time. At first, this period of time should be the same as your best time in your best stroke for 25 yards if you are under twelve, or for 50 yards if you are twelve or over. If you are under twelve and swim 25 yards of freestyle in 15 seconds, this would mean that you should repeat as many exercises as you can in 15 seconds. If you are over twelve and swim 50 yards in 30 seconds, repeat the exercise for 30 seconds.

When you increase the repetitions in an exercise by five or more, you are ready to move to the next level. Increase the length of the drill by 5 seconds for each level until you have reached your best time for 50 yards if you are under twelve, or for 100 yards if you are twelve or over.

Do the nine drills for endurance every day. Record each day on your DIARY FOR IMPROVEMENT IN ENDURANCE the time you spent on each drill and the number of times you were able to repeat the drill in the set time. Your chart should show a steady improvement both in repeats and in length of time.

DIARY FOR IMPROVEMENT IN ENDURANCE

DRILL		1	2	3	4	5	6	7	8	9	10	11	12	13	14	15	16	17	18	19	20	21	22	23	24	25	26	27	28	29	30	31
SIT-UPS	time																															
	no. of reps.																															
PUSH-UPS	time																															
	no. of reps.																															
STRAIGHT-ARM PULLOVERS	time																															
	no. of reps.																															
ARM ROTATOR	time																															
	no. of reps.																															
REVERSE CURLS	time																															
	no. of reps.																															
TOE RISE (RIGHT)	time																															
	no. of reps.																															
(LEFT)	time																															
	no. of reps.																															
BALL SQUEEZE (RIGHT)	time																															
	no. of reps.																															
(LEFT)	time																															
	no. of reps.																															
CAT LAPPERS	time																															
	no. of reps.																															
BENT-ARM EXTENDERS	time																															
	no. of reps.																															

DATE _____ month

Drill 1—Sit-Ups

Sit on the floor or pool deck with your knees bent. Have a partner hold your feet, or put them under a heavy chair or couch, to hold them down. See how many times you can go from a lying down to an upright sitting position.

Drill 2—Swimmers' Push-Ups

Take a push-up position with your body straight and your arms extended and holding your body off the floor. Your toes should be on a chair or a bed so that they are higher than your shoulders, or a partner can lift your knees. Do as many push-ups as you can in the time you are allowed (Fig. 60).

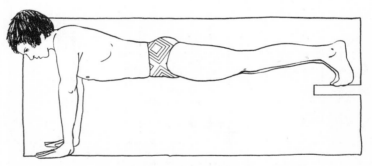

Fig. 60 / Swimmer's Push-Ups. Drill 2.

Drill 3—Straight-Arm Pullovers

Lie on your back with your legs crossed. Hold barbells that are 10–20 percent of your body weight. If you weigh 115 pounds, for instance, you should set your barbells at 15 or 20 pounds.

Start with your arms straight and stretched out on the floor above your head. Keep your arms straight while you lift the barbells until they are above your face. Then lower them over your head until they are just above the floor. Don't let them touch the floor before you lift them again. Repeat as many times as you can in the set time.

Drill 4—Arm Rotator
Lie on the floor on your back, holding the barbells above your head. Your elbows should be a little farther apart than your shoulder width. This time, bend your elbows and lift the barbells above your face with your elbows still on the floor. Lower them over your head until they are just above the floor. Continue to lift and lower the barbells without letting them touch the floor (Fig. 61).

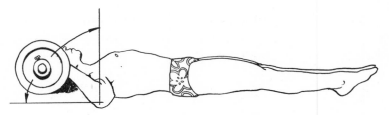

Fig. 61 / Arm Rotator. Drill 4.

Drill 5—Reverse Curls
Hold barbells that are from 30–40 percent of your body weight. If you weigh 115, you should set them at 40 pounds.

Hold them in front of you on your thighs with your arms straight and your palms turned toward your legs. Bend your elbows and bring the bar up to your shoulders. Lower it again to your thighs by extending your arms. Repeat.

Drill 6—Toe Rise

Stand with the ball of one foot on the edge of a stair, large book, or edge of the pool. Hold a stair railing, chair, or your partner for support. Stand on tiptoe. Then let your heel drop as low as possible. Do this drill with your right foot, then your left. Do it for speed. Try to do at least one toe rise per second.

Drill 7—Ball Squeeze

Hold a tennis ball or a small rubber ball in one hand. How many times can you squeeze the ball in the set time? Squeeze with your right hand first, then your left.

Drill 8—Cat Lappers

When you do this drill, you will look like a cat lapping milk.

Start in a push-up position. Your feet should be together on the floor. Your body and arms should be straight (Fig. 62a).

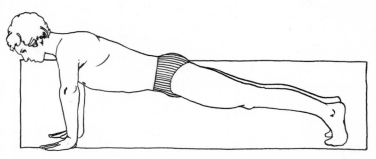

Fig. 62 / Cat Lappers. Drill 8. (a) Push-up position.

First, bend your arms and knees and move your head and body back toward your thighs by bending at your waist and hips (Fig. 62b). Keep your nose about 4 inches off the ground. When your head is as close to your knees as it can go, push forward with your legs, still keeping your head 4 inches off the ground.

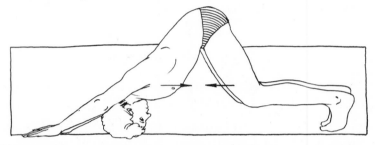

(b) Bring head and torso toward thighs; knees bend to bring thighs toward head and torso.

When your head is as far forward as it can go, lift it and look ahead (Fig. 62c). Straighten your arms to your original push-up position as you look forward. Drop your head down and move it back toward your feet again.

The greater distance you can move your head forward and back, the better this exercise will be for you.

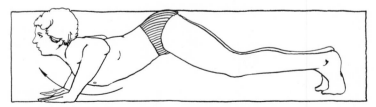

(c) Push forward, arch back, lift head.

Drill 9—Bent-Arm Extenders

Hold a barbell that is 30–40 percent of your body weight behind your head with your palms forward. You should be sitting or standing upright with your elbows pointing straight ahead.

Extend your arms and lift the barbells above your head. Repeat as many times as you can.

DRILLS FOR STRENGTH

Exercises to increase strength are more important during the latter half of the season. You should work on these drills for a set number of repetitions. You will try to increase your overload to become stronger. Increasing your strength will give you speed in the water.

You should do these drills every day. *Be sure that you have warmed up with lighter exercise before you begin.* This will help you avoid muscle strain.

On your DIARY FOR IMPROVEMENT IN STRENGTH AND FLEXIBILITY, record the number of repetitions, weight, or number of minutes as suggested for each of the drills. Keep your diaries for endurance and strength and flexibility legible and up-to-date so that you and your coach can see what progress you are making.

DIARY FOR IMPROVEMENT IN STRENGTH AND FLEXIBILITY

DRILLS FOR STRENGTH

		1 2 3 4 5 6 7 8 9 10 11 12 13 14 15 16 17 18 19 20 21 22 23 24 25 26 27 28 29 30 31
SIT-UPS	weight	
	no. of reps.	
PUSH-UPS	no. of reps.	
PULLOVERS	no. of reps.	
KNEE-KNOCKERS	total min.	
INSIDE)	total min.	
(OUTSIDE)	total min.	
STRAIGHT-ARM PUSH	total min.	
(PRESS DOWN)	total min.	
(PRESS UP)	total min.	
INNERS & OUTERS	total min.	
(IN)	total min.	
(OUT)	total min.	

DRILLS FOR FLEXIBILITY

HEEL-SITS	no. of min.	
WALL-LEANER	no. of reps.	
WALK-AROUNDS	no. of reps.	
CLIFF-HANGERS	no. of reps.	
TOWEL STRETCH	distance between hands	

DATE _____ month

Drill 1—Sit-Ups

Hold barbells or the biggest book you have in the house on your chest while you do sit-ups. Repeat thirty to fifty times. When you can do fifty sit-ups, increase the weight on your chest.

Drill 2—Push-Ups

Have your partner put pressure on your shoulders as you do your push-ups. The pressure can be increased as you become stronger. Try to work up to a push-up with someone light sitting on your back. Repeat fifteen to twenty-five times.

Drill 3—Locked Double-Arm Pullovers

Lie on your back with your arms locked above your head so that your right hand holds your left elbow and your left hand holds your right elbow.

Your partner should be above you in a push-up position, holding both your elbows against the floor or pool deck. You will try to lift your partner by raising your elbows until they

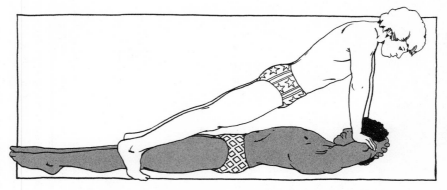

Fig. 63 / Locked Double-Arm Pullovers. Drill 3.

are above your shoulders. Lift ten to twenty times (Fig. 63).

If necessary, your partner can reduce the weight on your arms by putting one foot forward and shifting part of the weight to that leg.

Drill 4—Knee-Knockers

You and your partner should sit on the floor facing each other. Place your hands on the floor behind you and lean back. Your feet should be flat on the floor, your knees bent and against the inside of your partner's knees. Push out against your partner's knees while your partner pushes in against yours for 6 seconds, then rest for 4. Push out for 6 and rest for 4 seconds. Continue for 2 minutes. Change positions with your partner. Try to squeeze your partner's knees together for 6 seconds. Rest for 4. Squeeze and rest alternately for 2 more minutes (Fig. 64).

This exercise will strengthen the leg muscles you need for a strong breaststroke kick.

Fig. 64 / Knee-Knockers. Drill 4.

Drill 5—Straight-Arm Push

Lie on the floor or pool deck on your stomach with your arms extended above your head and your palms down. Your partner should lie on his or her back with hands extended above the head and palms up and touching yours. Press your palms down against your partner's hands for 6 seconds and rest for 4. Continue pressing and resting for 2 minutes. Exchange positions. Lie on your back and lift up against your partner's hands. Lift and rest for 2 more minutes.

Drill 6—Inners And Outers

Stand facing your partner. Reach out to your partner with your arms straight and the palms of your hands facing each other. Your thumbs will be pointing up. Your partner's palms will face away from each other. They should be against yours, with thumbs pointing down. Try to push your hands together while your partner pushes out. Again, push for 6 seconds and rest for 4. Continue for 2 minutes. Exchange positions and push out while your partner pushes in.

DRILLS FOR FLEXIBILITY

Flexibility exercises should be repeated every day of every year as long as you continue to train and as part of your warm-up before competition. Flexibility changes are gradual. Don't push too hard. You should feel stress—but not pain. A hot shower before your flexibility drills will help you relax your muscles and avoid strain.

ANKLE FLEXIBILITY

Drill 1—Heel-Sits

This drill is to increase ankle extension flexibility for improving your flutter kick and dolphin kick.

Kneel on both knees on the floor or pool deck. Now sit back on both feet with your toes pointed and turned in slightly or pigeon-toed. The tops of your feet should be against the floor or deck.

You can do heel-sits while studying or watching T.V. See if you can spend more and more time in this position without becoming uncomfortable.

Drill 2—Wall-Leaner

This drill will increase your ankle flection and improve your breaststroke kick.

Stand a distance equal to half your height away from a wall. Lean forward until the palms of your hands are against the wall with your fingers up. Keep your body straight as you lower it toward the floor by walking down the wall with your hands. Don't lift your heels from the floor! Repeat this drill ten times.

SHOULDER FLEXIBILITY

Drill 1—Walk-Arounds

Put the palm of your right hand on the wall at shoulder height. Push your left shoulder back and away from the wall. Walk in a circle until you feel your shoulder stretch. If you are very flexible, you may be able to turn far enough to see your right hand over your left shoulder.

Drill 2—Cliff-Hangers

With your back toward the wall, put your palms on the wall slightly above shoulder height. Move your hands so that they are a shoulder's width apart. Your fingers should point up (Fig. 65a).

Lower your body by bending your knees, and let it move back toward the wall. Your arms should be straight throughout the drill, and your hands should not move. Sit against the wall for a short time, and then stand up. Shake your arms and shoulders loose. Repeat five to ten times (Fig. 65b).

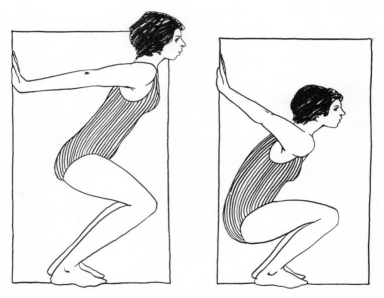

Fig. 65 / Cliff-Hangers. Drill 2. (a) Back toward wall, palms on wall. (b) Bend knees, lower body toward wall, keep palms on wall.

Drill 3—Towel Stretch

Hold a towel with both hands in front of you with your arms straight. Hold it as wide as you can. Keep your arms straight as you swing the towel over your head until it is behind your back. Gradually narrow the distance between your hands. You may someday be able to hold them as close together as the width of your shoulders.

Chapter Eleven
PREPARING FOR COMPETITION

You have learned and refined your strokes with drills. You have trained hard to become physically fit. Now you are ready to test yourself in competition.

Most competitive seasons begin with dual meets—swim meets in which one team competes against another. Team spirit will be high as each swimmer tries to add to the team's score. Most dual meets last from two to four hours.

Later in the season your team may enter invitational or championship meets. These meets are much longer, most often lasting two full days. Since there are usually many swimmers in each event, the events are divided into heats of six or eight swimmers. Swimmers are placed in heats according to their entry times—their best time for the season. This method of placing swimmers according to their ability is called *seeding*.

In many large meets there may be preliminaries in the morning and afternoon. You will then swim for times that you hope may qualify you to swim again in the finals later in the afternoon or in the evening. The fastest times in each event will qualify for championship and consolation brackets. How you swim in the finals will determine your place and award.

Other meets may have timed finals instead of preliminaries and finals. In timed finals, you will swim only once in each event you have entered. Your official time will determine your place. In these meets, heats are seeded so that swimmers with the slowest entry times swim first and those with the fastest times are in the final heat.

There is always some physical and emotional stress in competition, but there are ways you can prepare yourself for a meet to keep this stress to a minimum. Less stress will help keep your storage battery of energy charged for your swimming events.

TAKE ALONG

You should have a travel bag to carry most of the things you will take to swim meets. On the outside of the bag, tape a list of all the things you may need at the meet. Check your list

Fig. 66 / Swim Meet Check List.

before you leave home and any time you go to or from the pool area (Fig. 66).

Your list should include:

1. Two swim suits
2. Two towels
3. Team sweat suit
4. Any medication (eye drops, ear drops, chapstick, etc.)
5. Things to help you relax (cards, books, games)
6. Snack food (oranges, hard candy, thermos of soup, sandwich, cookies)
7. Extra sweat shirt, jacket, or other warm clothing depending on weather
8. Sleeping bag or blankets for resting and warmth
9. Something warm for your feet

And for summer meets in outdoor pools:

10. Something to make shade (tarp, beach umbrella, etc.)
11. Suntan lotion

Pack your bag the day before the meet. Put it and your sleeping bag or blankets and any other items that don't fit in your bag together so that you can find them easily the next morning. Being prepared and ready to go will eliminate one source of stress. You can feel secure in knowing that you have everything you will need at the meet. And the check list will not only help you remember what you need to take, but will help you remember to bring it home.

It is wise to have your name on your bag and name tags on

all your belongings. If something is misplaced or left at the pool, it can then be easily identified and returned to you.

FOOD

Since you will be eating lightly just before and during the swim meet, you will want to have a big meal the night before. A good dinner will help you sleep and let you get along with less food the next day. What you eat is not too important. Eat what you like, and as much as you want.

If you will *not* be swimming an event within three hours after breakfast, you can eat all you want the morning of the meet. A meal that is high in carbohydrates is good. Pancakes or waffles with syrup are a favorite of many swimmers.

During the meet you can eat often, but only in small quantities. You should feel neither hungry nor full at any time. Nibbling food or sucking hard candy helps relieve tension.

Oranges are an excellent food to take to a meet. Not only are they easily digested, but they help reduce mucus that may accumulate in your mouth and throat. They will also control the desire to eat large quantities of food.

Hot soups in a thermos are easily digested and help you relax. If you take sandwiches for lunch, be sure you don't eat more than half a sandwich at a time.

At an invitational or championship meet, there is normally a snack bar. Jello or hot soup are good light snacks that you will usually find at a swim meet snack bar.

CONSERVING ENERGY

Think of your body as a storage battery. There are two types of energy that it needs to operate at its very best— physical energy and nervous energy.

PHYSICAL ENERGY

You should store physical energy for three nights and two days before a meet. For those nights, you should go to bed an hour earlier than usual. Rest does not mean that you must sleep if you are not sleepy. A quiet hour of reading may do nearly as much good.

Your daytime routine may be much the same as usual. Most coaches will continue training programs. But you should avoid anything outside of your routine that will drain a large amount of energy from your storage supply.

The night before the meet you may be restless and have trouble getting to sleep. Don't worry! If you have had the rest you need the two nights and days before, this may only mean that your battery is fully charged. Rest. Relax. Read for a while if you like. The next morning you will leave for the meet with a full supply of physical energy.

NERVOUS ENERGY

Because of the excitement of a meet, you will probably not feel tired even if your storage of physical energy is low. Your nervous energy will keep you going, but your lack of physical energy will hurt your performance. To swim your best, you need a ready supply of both physical and nervous energy.

Your nervous energy might be compared to the steam from boiling water. Your excitement will keep the water boiling, but if the steam is not controlled, it will go in every direction, like steam from an open saucepan, and accomplish very little. If the steam, or energy, is saved for your swimming events, it will have power like the steam in the teakettle that makes the kettle whistle.

One of the most important things you can learn is how to conserve and control your nervous energy. Learn to relax as much as possible. Sucking hard candy, reading, playing cards or quiet games are good distractions that will help relieve the tensions of competition and conserve your nervous energy. Walk! Never run! Move slowly. Even talk more slowly and quietly. Remember . . . the steam that stays under control will be there for you to use at the sound of the starter's gun.

TRAVEL

One advantage of being on a swim team is that you will travel, meet new friends, and see new places. You will benefit the most from these trips if you find out beforehand what places of interest the area has to offer. Plan your time so that you can visit museums, historic landmarks, scenic attractions, etc. There may be time for sight-seeing before or after the meet each day or between preliminaries and finals.

Plan to arrive at the pool at least two hours before the meet is scheduled to start. Then add an extra hour to your travel time for the unexpected—a flat tire, parking problems, difficulty finding the pool, etc. Worry about being late will drain your storehouse of energy.

Nonstop trips of any length are tiring. Plan your trip so that you can get out of the car and stretch your legs from time to time. Stop at a park, or at a restaurant for a snack. Or visit scenic or historical points of interest along the way. If there is enough room in the car, or if you are in a station wagon, stretch your legs out or lie down for part of the trip.

Playing games along the way will help you relax. Look for out-of-state license plates. Find the letters of the alphabet one by one on roadside signs. Or play Twenty Questions.

If you travel with someone other than your own family, be sure that your parents and your coach know who you will be with and where you can be reached when you are away from the meet.

MENTAL PREPARATION

You can begin to prepare yourself mentally a week or more before the meet. Your coach can help you with information about the meet, the pool, and the city or town in which it will be held. Find out from your coach the address of the pool, its special characteristics, and the best route for getting there. Record the information on your SWIM MEET INFORMATION SHEET. This will help keep differences in the pool from being a distraction and will minimize worry about accommodations, route, starting times, etc.

When you arrive at the pool, get a heat sheet and complete your SWIM MEET INFORMATION SHEET by filling out the last two items—your heat numbers and the approximate time you will be swimming each event.

Keep the sheet handy in your travel bag during the entire meet, and check it often. After the meet, put it in your swim team notebook so you can refer to it the next time you compete at the same pool.

The heat sheet will also tell you if you are listed in the events you had planned to enter. Mistakes are sometimes made when heats are seeded. If you are not listed in an event you thought you were swimming, tell your coach immediately so that the records can be checked. Only your coach can see that a mistake is corrected.

Know your competition. The heat sheet will tell you what other swimmers are entered in your events. You may have competed with many of them before, but there may be some unfamiliar names. Entry times will tell you a lot about the swimmers you don't know. They will give you a good idea of how much competition you'll be facing in your events.

SWIM MEET INFORMATION SHEET

MEET _____ DATES _____
POOL _____ _____ _____ _____
       name   address   city   state
BEST ROUTE TO POOL _____
_____

POOL DESCRIPTION: LENGTH __ NO. OF LANES _____
      STARTING BLOCKS _____ GUTTERS _____
      LANE MARKINGS _____ LIGHTING _____
      TIMING EQUIPMENT _____
HOUSING _____ _____ _____
        motel   address   rates

   _____ _____ _____
        motel   address   rates

   _____ _____ _____
        motel   address   rates
TRAILER PARK _____ _____ _____
                address   rates
CAMPING _____
POOL OPEN FOR WARM-UP _____ _____ _____
         day   time   day   time   day   time
MEET STARTING TIME _____ _____ _____
         day   time   day   time   day   time

EVENTS ENTERED	DAY	EVENT NUMBER	HEAT NUMBER	APPROX. TIME
_____	_____	_____	_____	_____
_____	_____	_____	_____	_____
_____	_____	_____	_____	_____
_____	_____	_____	_____	_____
_____	_____	_____	_____	_____
_____	_____	_____	_____	_____
_____	_____	_____	_____	_____

WARM-UP

Most pools will open for warm-ups an hour to an hour and a half before the start of the meet. You should be ready to go in the water as soon as the pool opens. Your performance in your events will be best if you have a complete, three-phase warm-up.

Phase I—Get Used To The Pool

As soon as warm-ups begin, get into the pool and make yourself as familiar with it as you can. Get used to the temperature of the water. Try out the starting blocks for both forward and back starts. Check the lane markers on the bottom of the pool. Most lines end 5 feet before the wall, but you will sometimes find pools where this is not true. Try some turns. How does the lighting affect your view of the wall? How are the gutters for breaststroke and butterfly turns?

You will feel familiar with the pool after fifteen to twenty minutes swimming laps very slowly. You can swim drills, kicking, pulling, or whole strokes. Don't swim faster than 60 percent of your best effort.

Phase II—Build-Up Swims

By reviewing your speed stroke and skills during the warm-up, you can program your mind and muscles like a computer. Tuning up just before the meet begins will help get you ready for your events.

Do build-up swims as you practiced in your drills for each stroke you will swim that day. Combine these with practice on turns. Work on these skills for ten to thirty minutes.

Phase III—Timed Sprints

For the last 15 to 30 minutes before the start of the meet, you should do short, timed sprints. You will start from the blocks and swim 25 or 50 yards or meters while your coach or an assistant times you with a stopwatch. Swim fast, but try to keep your muscles relaxed.

In large meets the pool will be very crowded during the warm-up session. You may be forced to swim the first two phases of your drills slower than you had planned. Don't worry, but give yourself a longer warm-up. Your timed sprints will sensitize your muscles for speed.

Chapter Twelve
THE SWIM MEET

"SWIMMERS CLEAR THE POOL!" a voice booms over the loudspeaker.

The warm-up is over. Young people, large and small, climb onto the deck and search for towels they have left nearby. Within minutes the pool is empty.

Swimmers return to the area where their teams are gathered and slip into colorful sweat suits. The resting area is bright with clusters of reds, blues, greens, oranges, and purples as team members sit together waiting for their events to be called.

THE POOL

The pool, which was so recently churning with hundreds of arms and legs, is now flat and calm. It is divided into lanes by strings of floats called *lane lines*. At one end of each lane is a starting block rising above the deck at the edge of the pool no more than 30 inches above the level of the water.

Dark lines on the bottom of the pool mark the centers of the lanes, but they stop 5 feet from each end of the pool.

These lane markers help swimmers swim straight and warn them when they are approaching the wall.

A brightly colored string of flags is stretched above the water 15 feet inside each end of the pool. These are backstroke flags. They help backstrokers know when they are nearing the wall.

Forty-five feet away from the starting blocks, a rope called the *false start line* hangs across the water. In case of a false start, the rope will be dropped as a signal to swimmers to stop and return to the starting blocks (Fig. 67).

THE OFFICIALS

Beside the pool, white-clad officials are busy preparing for the start of the meet. The meet referee makes sure that they all have their assignments. The referee has the responsibility for the operation of the meet and must make all final decisions. If a swimmer feels that an official's decision is wrong, an appeal can be made to the meet referee, but this must be done by the coach. Swimmers or parents of swimmers must not appeal directly to any official.

The starter is loading the starting gun with blanks and checking to see that it is in good working order. He or she will have control of the start of each race and will determine false starts. Turn judges take their places at either end of the pool, while stroke judges wait for the first race to begin. The turn judges will see that swimmers touch the wall and that no illegal turns are made. Stroke judges will make sure that all strokes are done correctly according to regulations.

At the end of each lane, three timers wait by the starting block. It is their job to check take-offs in relays and make

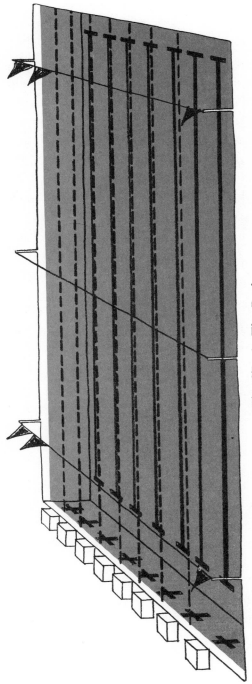

Fig. 67 / The Pool.

———— = LANE LINES.

🚩🚩 = BACKSTROKE FLAGS.

◢◣ = STARTING BLOCKS.

⌐ = FALSE START LINE.

T = LANE MARKERS.

✛ = TARGET MARKS.

sure that swimmers are in the right lanes and heats as well as to time the swimmers in their lane. They may use a stopwatch to take times, although they more often use hand-held electronic timers. Or the pool may be equipped with an electronic button system. Timers then press a button as swimmers touch the wall. There are three stopwatches, electronic timers, or buttons for each lane.

The most accurate method of timing swimmers is an electronic touch pad at the end of the pool. A fingertip touch as the swimmer swims into the finish records the time to 1/100th of a second.

"WILL THE SWIMMERS IN EVENT NUMBER ONE, HEATS ONE, TWO, AND THREE PLEASE REPORT TO THE CLERK-OF-COURSE," the loudspeaker blares.

The clerk-of-course checks names against the heat sheet and seats swimmers in rows in the bull pen, or ready area, to wait for their race.

"SWIMMERS IN EVENT ONE, HEAT ONE, PLEASE REPORT TO THE STARTING BLOCKS."

A hush falls over the crowd. The meet is about to begin.

THE RACE

Before the meet, you and your coach will have worked out a race plan. If your event is 100 yards or more, you will have a plan for the pace you should set. You will divide your race into 25-, 50-, or 100-yard or meter distances. The race plan will include a time goal for each distance.

Your times for each part of the race are called *splits.* Your splits will tell you whether or not you have paced yourself as you planned. Get your splits from your coach after each

COMPETITION RECORD SHEET FOR _____ meet _____ dates

	EVENT _____ stroke-distance	EVENT _____ stroke-distance	EVENT _____ stroke-distance	EVENT _____ stroke-distance	EVENT _____ stroke-distance	EVENT _____ stroke-distance
Splits						
Were my splits as planned?						
Did some of my muscles get more tired than others? Why?						
Was my warm-up adequate?						
Did I gain or lose on starts? On turns?						
Did I meet my competition with confidence and a plan?						
Where do I need to improve?						
What part of my training will help me improve?						
Comments						

race and record them on your COMPETITION RECORD SHEET.

Just before and during your event, remember any tips your coach has given you to improve your time. Use them in your race.

When each of your events is over, answer the questions about the race on your COMPETITION RECORD SHEET. The answers will give both you and your coach an insight into the sort of training that will best improve your future performances.

AVOID DISQUALIFICATION

If you have learned your strokes and turns correctly, you will seldom be disqualified. Most disqualifications result from being careless, thoughtless, or overexcited. The most common disqualifications can be avoided if you think before you act.

Never get into the pool until the event before yours is over and the referee or starter has given swimmers permission to get into the water. This rule is most often broken in long-distance races or relays.

False starts may be caused by getting into position so fast that you lose your balance. And be sure to concentrate on the starter's gun. Ignore distracting sounds or shouts.

Disqualifications on turns are most often caused either by excitement, failure to get used to a new pool situation, or bad habits from using illegal or sloppy turns in practice.

Don't miss an event! Failure to report on time can disqualify you from that event or from the entire meet, depending on the meet and meet referee.

WHAT IS WINNING?

Too many people think of winning as being first. There are more important ways of winning. Winning is accomplishing. Many things can make you a winner. These are a few:

1. You followed your race plan.
2. You had a good start.
3. You did your best turn.
4. You finished the race strong.
5. You tried your hardest.
6. You learned something about yourself.
7. You were responsible for getting yourself to all your events on time.
8. You made a new friend.
9. You had fun.
10. You swam a lifetime best.

If you swam a lifetime best, you accomplished something more important than a first place. It was a positive measure of your improvement. Keep a record of your lifetime bests for each event you swim, noting the meet and the date that it was made. Record them on the chart for LIFETIME BESTS in pencil. You'll change them often as you continue to improve.

LIFETIME BESTS

Name _____   Team _____

STROKE	DISTANCE	MEET	DATE	TIME
FREESTYLE	50 yards	_____	_____	_____
	50 meters	_____	_____	_____
	100 yards	_____	_____	_____
	100 meters	_____	_____	_____
	200 yards	_____	_____	_____
	200 meters	_____	_____	_____
	_____	_____	_____	_____
	_____	_____	_____	_____
BACKSTROKE	50 yards	_____	_____	_____
	50 meters	_____	_____	_____
	100 yards	_____	_____	_____
	100 meters	_____	_____	_____
	200 yards	_____	_____	_____
	200 meters	_____	_____	_____
BREASTSTROKE	50 yards	_____	_____	_____
	50 meters	_____	_____	_____
	100 yards	_____	_____	_____
	100 meters	_____	_____	_____
	200 yards	_____	_____	_____
	200 meters	_____	_____	_____
BUTTERFLY	50 yards	_____	_____	_____
	50 meters	_____	_____	_____
	100 yards	_____	_____	_____
	100 meters	_____	_____	_____
	200 yards	_____	_____	_____
	200 meters	_____	_____	_____

Name   Team

STROKE	DISTANCE	MEET	DATE	TIME
INDIVIDUAL	100 yards	_____	_____	_____
MEDLEY	100 meters	_____	_____	_____
	200 yards	_____	_____	_____
	200 meters	_____	_____	_____
	400 yards	_____	_____	_____
	400 meters	_____	_____	_____

Chapter Thirteen

WHAT MAKES A SUCCESSFUL SWIMMER?

What are your goals? Do you want to be at the top of your age group on your team? In your city? In your state? In the nation? Perhaps you dream of someday setting a world record or winning a gold medal at the Olympics.

The road to success is not an easy one to follow. It is a steep road, paved with disappointments, sacrifice, and a great deal of hard work. Is it worth the effort? Ask any swimmer who has made it to the top. The answer will be a resounding "yes."

If you really want to be a successful swimmer, you already have one quality you will need—the *desire* to succeed. The greater your desire, the greater will be your chance for success. There are other things, too, that will help you reach your goal.

KEEP A HEALTHY BODY

In order to get the most good from your training, you should be sure that you are eating a balanced diet and getting enough rest.

Foods that are most important in your diet are those that develop cells and help your physical growth. Proteins found in meat, fish, poultry, eggs, cheese, and milk help build muscles. Liver is an especially good food for swimmers because, in addition to building muscles, it helps build red blood cells.

Vegetables contain vitamins that you will need. The dark or bright-colored vegetables, such as spinach, carrots, and beets, are richest in vitamins. Swimmers who are in heavy training may take food supplements to add extra vitamins and minerals to their diets.

A consistent routine of rest is important. You should have a regular time each day for going to bed and for getting up. If you are in a twice-a-day training program, it is doubly important that you get plenty of rest to keep your resistance to infection high.

Your body, like a storage battery, may sometimes be drawn down in energy with heavy training. You will feel tired. Your times may be slower than usual. This is a warning signal that your body needs more rest.

Get more sleep at night. Stay relaxed during the day by doing things slowly, being less active, and engaging in quiet activities like reading or watching television. Recharge your batteries with physical energy. If you let yourself remain in a "drawn-down" condition, you will not only hurt your swimming performance but you will be much more susceptible to colds or other illnesses.

In about three months, if there are no setbacks from illness, and if you are consistent in eating habits, resting, and training, there should be a permanent change in your physical make-up. You will reach a higher level of stamina and strength. What you do today, you will be tomorrow.

KEEP A POSITIVE ATTITUDE

We all remember the story of the little engine who puffed her way to the top of the mountain saying, "I think I can! I think I can! I think I can!" The swimmer who succeeds must have the same sort of a positive attitude—the same self-confidence.

The path to success will not be a steady upward climb. There will be valleys between the peaks and disappointments along the way. Champions learn to regard their wins and losses not as isolated moments of victory or defeat but as merely a part of their long-range plan. They are sure enough of themselves—of their own ability and dedication—to know that any goal they strive for is possible.

HAVE THE DESIRE TO LEARN

The swimmer who succeeds will welcome any new idea that may help improve a stroke, a start, or a turn. These swimmers are called *coachable.* They are patient and listen carefully to instructions, then think about using those instructions to improve their swimming skills. Any suggestion from their coach is remembered and applied to all their training from that time on.

WORK HARD

Swimmers who continue to improve swim greater distances and push for higher percentage efforts in training. They realize that when they are tired, their bodies are being challenged, and it is at this point that they will improve. They know this is the only way they will reach their greatest potential.

This attitude toward training helps establish work patterns that will stay with them throughout their lives. Champions never quit. When the going gets tough, they get tougher.

BE WILLING TO SACRIFICE

Swimmers who have succeeded as competitors will tell you that the road to the top was not easy to climb. They have made more sacrifices, large and small, along the way than they can even remember. Do *you* really want to succeed? Are you willing to make sacrifices?

Your alarm rings. You reach over sleepily and shut it off. It's 5:00 A.M. A cold rain is beating hard against the window, but your bed is snug and warm. There's a six o'clock workout before school. The coach said no one *had* to come, but he'd be there to give extra help to those who did. You know that more work on your starts and turns will be important in the next meet.

You can pull the covers back over your shoulders and

sleep for another hour and a half. Or you can go out in the dark and the rain and ride your bike ten blocks to the pool.

It's Friday night. There's a meet tomorrow. You have your bag packed and everything's ready to go. You've picked out a book and are about to go to your room and read until bedtime. Then the phone rings. It's your best friend.

"Guess what?" your friend says. "Pat's invited all us kids over tonight for a big party. I'll stop by your house in ten minutes and we can go together."

"I've got a swim meet tomorrow."

"Oh, come on! Everybody'll be there. And that includes somebody I know you'd really like to see."

"I'd better not."

"Oh, you and those dumb swim meets. You're getting to be a real drag. Pretty soon everybody'll give you up and you'll never get asked to a party."

"I don't think . . ."

"Just for an hour or two. You can still get home in time to get enough of your stupid sleep. I'll be by in ten minutes."

How important will that rest be tomorrow when your relay team tries to set a new meet record?

Are you willing to make sacrifices? To work hard? To keep trying? Success in swimming is something you must earn for yourself. No one can do it for you. The good feeling you have when you know you've done your best and reached your goal belongs only to you. The choice is yours.

SWIM TEAM VOCABULARY

AAU. Initials for the Amateur Athletic Union, an organization that regulates most amateur sports, outside of high school and college, in the United States. Most age-group swimmers are registered members of the AAU, and nearly all age-group swim meets are governed by AAU rules.

AGE GROUP. Under AAU rules, swimmers are divided into the following age groups: eight and under, nine and ten, eleven and twelve, thirteen and fourteen, fifteen through seventeen, and senior.

ANCHOR. The swimmer to swim the last leg on a relay team.

ASSOCIATION. The geographical regions into which the United States has been divided by the AAU.

AWARDS STAND. A platform where swimmers stand to be recognized and to receive their awards.

BACKSTROKE. Another name given to the back crawl stroke.

BACKSTROKE FLAGS. A line of flags stretched across the pool 15 feet inside each end to help backstrokers know when they are approaching the wall.

BLOCKS. A term used by swimmers to refer to the starting blocks from which they begin a race.

BROKEN SWIMS. A form of interval training in which repeat swims are broken into shorter swims. A 200-meter repeat may be broken into 4 times 50, 2 times 100, or 100, 50, 50. Swimmers try to swim progressively faster with each part of a broken swim.

BULL PEN. An area where swimmers assemble before their event, are assigned to their heats, and wait for their heat to be called to the blocks. It is sometimes called the *ready area.*

CHAMPIONSHIP MEET. An open meet where any AAU team can compete to determine event and team winners.

CHIEF TIMER. An official in charge of all timers. He or she assigns at least two, but usually three, timers to each lane to determine the time of each swimmer in that lane.

CLERK-OF-COURSE. An official to whom swimmers must report before their event in an invitational or championship meet. It is the job of the clerk-of-course to see that swimmers are in the bull pen, separated into heats, and ready for their event.

COACH. A person qualified to direct the training and skill development of swimmers. He or she is in charge of all operations of a swim team, such as training and meet schedules, meet entries, and purchase of equipment. But, above all, a coach is a friend who helps and encourages swimmers to reach their greatest potential.

DISQUALIFICATION. A stroke, turn, or start done incorrectly according to AAU rules.

DUAL MEET. A swimming contest between two teams.

ENTRY. A card containing the swimmer's name, event entered, team, AAU number, age, and best time in that event. This card is submitted by a coach or swimmer and used for assigning heats and lanes for a swim meet.

ENTRY FEE. A fee charged for each entry in an invitational or championship meet. Entry fees help the host team pay for awards and other meet expenses.

FALSE START. If a swimmer moves or leaves the starting blocks too soon, a false start is called. It is signaled by two shots from the starter's gun. AAU rules provide that anyone who false starts after two false starts from the field of competitors, is disqualified.

FALSE START LINE. A rope that is dropped across the pool in the event of a false start. It is a signal for swimmers to stop and return to their blocks.

FINALS. Invitational and championship meets are sometimes divided into preliminaries and finals. The swimmers with the fastest time in the preliminaries (usually six or eight, depending on the size of the pool) will swim in the championship bracket. Those with the next fastest times will swim in the consolation bracket of the finals. The last-place swimmer in the championship bracket will place higher than the first-place swimmer in the consolation bracket regardless of their times.

FITNESS TRAINING. Training to improve heart action and blood circulation so that a swimmer can swim longer distances with greater speed for less effort.

FLIP. To make a flip turn.

FLIP TURN. A somersault turn. The fastest turn used in the front crawl stroke and backstroke; used by all top swimmers.

FREESYTLE. Another name for the front crawl stroke.

FREESTYLE RELAY. A race in which four swimmers swim freestyle in succession. Each swimmer swims the same distance—usually 50 or 100 meters or yards.

GRAB START. A front start in which swimmers hold onto the starting blocks and use their hands as well as feet to push off. It is the fastest of all front starts.

HEAD SCORER. Official in charge of recording race results to determine individual and team scores.

HEAT. A division of all swimmers entered in an event and seeded according to their entry times.

HEAT SHEET. A program listing the names, teams, entry times, and lane assignments of the swimmers entered in a meet.

I. M. An abbreviation most often used by swimmers when referring to the individual medley (see below).

INDIVIDUAL MEDLEY. A race in which a competitor swims an equal distance of each of the four competitive strokes in the following order: butterfly, backstroke, breaststroke, and freestyle.

INTERVAL TRAINING. A training method in which a set distance is repeated with a set rest interval between each swim.

INVITATIONAL. A swim meet sponsored by a team or organization in which three or more teams are invited to participate.

KICK. A training technique in which feet and legs are the only force used to propel a swimmer through the water.

KINESTHESIA. The sense that makes you aware of your muscles and how they move.

KINESTHETIC FEEDBACK. An awareness of your movements, which tells you how your muscles can work best for you.

LANE LINES. Floats that run the length of the pool to mark the boundaries of each lane and to calm the waves. The last 5–10 feet are usually a different color to alert swimmers that they are approaching the wall.

LANE MARKERS. Dark lines on the bottom of the pool which mark the center of each lane and end 5 feet from the wall. The lines help swimmers swim straight and warn them when they are close to the wall.

LAP. Two lengths of the pool—down and back.

LONG COURSE. A pool which is 50 meters long is called a long-course pool. A race held in such a pool can establish long-course and world records.

MEDLEY RELAY. A relay in which four swimmers swim one of each of the four competitive strokes. The order is alphabetical: backstroke, breaststroke, butterfly, and freestyle.

NATIONAL AGE-GROUP RECORD. The fastest time ever recorded in the nation for a particular event and age group.

NATIONALS. The meet usually referred to when swimmers speak of "the nationals" is the National AAU Championship. It is open to any swimmer twelve or over who can meet the qualifying times. However, there are also collegiate national championships for university swimmers.

OFFICIAL. One of the many people needed to carry on the operation of a swim meet. Most officials are parents of the swimmers and volunteer their help.

OLYMPICS. The Olympic Games are held every four years to test the best amateur athletes in the world. To swim in the Olympics is one of the greatest honors a swimmer can achieve.

OPEN TURN. A turn in which the swimmer's head is kept above the surface of the water, allowing a breath to be taken during the turn. This turn is most often used in the breaststroke and butterfly.

OVERLOADING. In the learning process, overloading sensitizes arms, legs, or coordination by putting increased stress on a part of the stroke. In training, overloading forces swimmers to work harder and thereby helps them reach a higher level of fitness.

PACE CLOCK. A large clock with a second hand used at the end of a pool for training. It helps swimmers clock their own times.

PRELIMINARIES OR PRELIMS. Invitational or championship meets are sometimes divided into preliminaries, usually called prelims, and finals. Preliminary times of all contestants are ranked to determine which will qualify for the finals.

PROPULSION. Forces which drive a swimmer through the water.

PSYCHE SHEET. A term often used by swimmers to refer to a heat sheet, or a listing according to entry times of all swimmers entered in each event.

PULL. A training technique in which hands and arms are the only force used to propel a swimmer through the water.

QUALIFYING TIME. A standard set by a meet director for each event. A swimmer must have equaled or bettered that time to be qualified to enter that event.

RECORD. The fastest time recorded in a particular event. There are many kinds of records, such as world records (the fastest times ever recorded in the world in the events), Olympic records (the fastest times in an Olympics), American records (the fastest times in

America). There are also several types of age-group records that are set for a particular age group as well as for an event. Age-group records can be national, association, state, meet, or team.

RECORDER. An official who writes down the times clocked for the swimmers on his or her lane.

RECOVERY. The action which returns the arms or legs to the starting position, where they can again support and propel the swimmer.

RUNNER. A helper who takes official results from timers and judges to the head scorers' table.

SEEDING. A method by which swimmers are assigned lanes and heats according to entry times. Swimmers with the fastest times swim last, and the center lanes are the fastest in each heat.

SENSITIZATION. A special technique using stroke drills that prepare you to swim your own natural stroke.

SHORT COURSE. A pool which is 25 yards in length is called a short-course pool. A race held in such a pool can establish short-course records.

SPLITS. The division of a race into equal parts of 25, 50, or 100 yards or meters. Splits can tell how well a swimmer has swum a race or a leg of a relay.

SPRINT. The shortest race in each stroke.

START. A gun fired to signal the beginning of a race.

STARTER. The official who has control of the start of each race and determines false starts.

STARTING BLOCK. A platform at the end of each lane for swimmers to use to start a race.

STOPWATCH. A watch that can be started and stopped to time a swimmer's race. Hand-held electronic timers are sometimes used instead of stopwatches. They can give times to 1/100th of a second and splits for a race or relay.

STROKE JUDGE. An official who watches swimmer's strokes to see that they are done correctly according to the rules.

TARGET MARK. Usually a black square on wall at the end of each lane to aid swimmers in making turns.

TEAM SWEATS. Colorful pants and jackets to keep a swimmer warm and comfortable between events. They are usually in team colors and help identify the team to which the swimmer belongs.

TIME. The time from start to finish that a swimmer takes to swim a set distance. It is an objective way to record improvement.

TIMED FINALS. Timed finals are often used at invitational and championship meets where many swimmers are entered. Swimmers swim only once. Places and awards are determined by times.

TIMER. An official who takes the time of each swimmer in the lane to which he or she is assigned. There are usually three timers on each lane.

TIME TRIALS. Races within a team to establish qualifying times or to measure progress.

TURN JUDGE. An official who stands at the end of a lane and watches swimmers' turns to see that they are done correctly according to the rules.

WARM-UP. Usually an hour to an hour and a half before the start of a meet when the pool is open to participants. It is a time for swimmers to accustom themselves to the pool, to practice starts and turns, and to work with their coaches on their race plans. It is also a term used for the tune-up period before a team training session.

Index

Index

Amateur Athletic Union (AAU), 37
ankle, 20–22, 143
arms, *see* forces, propelling
attitude, 171

backstroke, 50
 breathing in, 50
 build-up swims for, 57–58
 drills for, 50–58
 finding own stroke for, 51–55
 kick for, 50
 refining stroke for, 55–58
 start in, 97–101
 turn in, 108–112
 warm-ups for, 58
 see also forces, propelling
balance, 27–28
body in water, 19–34
breaststroke, 60–61
 breathing in, 60
 build-up swims for, 67–68
 drills for, 61–68
 finding own stroke for, 61–66
 kick for, 22, 23, 60
 refining stroke for, 66–67
 start in, 93–96
 turn in, 112–118
 warm-ups for, 68
 see also forces, propelling
breathing, 29; *see also specific strokes*
buoyancy, 25–27

butterfly, 70
 breathing in, 70
 build-up swims for, 80–81
 drills for, 70–81
 finding own stroke for, 72–77
 kick for, 70
 refining stroke for, 77–81
 start in, 93–97
 turn in, 112–118
 warm-ups for, 81
 see also forces, propelling

charts
 competition record sheet, 163–164
 distance training graph, 126–127
 endurance improvement diary, 132–133
 guide for water training, 124–125
 lifetime bests, 165–167
 percentage of effort, 122–124
 personal profile, 20–21
 quality of training graph, 128–129
 strength and flexibility improvement diary, 138–139
 swim meet information sheet, 153–155
clerk-of-course, 162
competition

competition (cont.):
  energy conservation for, 151–152
  equipment for, 148–150
  food consumption and, 150
  preparing for, 147–157
  travel and, 152–153
  warm-up for, 156–157
crawl, front, 41–43
  breathing in, 43
  build-up swims for, 48
  drills for, 43–48
  finding own stroke for, 43–47
  kick for, 20–22, 30
  refining stroke for, 47–48
  warm-ups for, 48
  see also forces, propelling

diary, *see* charts
diet, *see* food
disqualification, 164
drills, 36–39, 120–121
  Arm Rotator, 135
  Back Dolphin Swim, 72
  backstroke, 50–58
  Ball Squeeze, 136
  Bent-Arm Extenders, 138
  Boat Launching, 100
  Boiling-Water Kick, 44, 45
  breaststroke, 61–68
  Broken-Leg Dolphin Kick, 77–78
  Broken-Wing Recovery, 73–74
  Bronco-Busting Arm Pull, 63
  Bronco-Busting Cymbal Player, 64–65
  butterfly, 70–81
  Butterfly Scooter, 74–75
  Cat Lappers, 136–137
  Cliff Hangers, 144
  code for (L, T, S, X), 39
  Crossover Pulling, 46–47
  Cup Of Water, 56
  Cymbals, 54

Dive And Reach, 88
Dive And Stretch, 88–89
Dive Over Kickboard, 101
Dolphin Swim, 72
Dolphin With Arms Extended, 74
Dolphin With Kickboard, 73
Drop And Push, 89–90
Drop-And-Push On Blocks, 90–91
Drop, Feather, And Push, 100–101, 110
endurance, 131–138
Feet-First Float, 64
flexibility, 142–145
Flipper, 111
front crawl, 43–48
grab start, freestyle, 89–92
Hand And Heel Touch, 63
Hands Locked Over Head, 53
Head Above Water, 47
Head Drop, 88
Heads-Up Butterfly, 79
Heads-Up Kick, 78
Heels And Chin, 65
Heels And Hips, Head Up, 66–67
Heels And Hips With Kickboard, 61–62
Heels And Hips Without Kickboard, 62–63
Heels, Chin, And Breathe, 66
Heel-Sits, 143
Hip Popper, 76–77
Hydroplane, 48
Inners And Outers, 142
Kick And Count, 52
Kickboard Kick-Out, 107
Kickboard Over Head, 52–53
Kickboard Over Knees, 52
Knee-Knockers, 141
Lane Line Drive, 94–95

Left Hand, Right Hand Kickboard, 106–107
Locked Double-Arm Pullovers, 140–141
One-Arm Pull Without Kickboard, 75
One-Arm Swim, 53–54
Overlapping Feet, 67
Periscope Up, 79
Pivot In Place, Face In Water, 117
Pivot In Place, Head Above Water, 115–116
Pull-Out For Breaststroke, 95
Pull-Out For Butterfly, 95–97
Pull-Out For Freestyle, 91–92
Push-Ups, 140
Reverse Curls, 135
Rowboat, 54
Scooter With Best Kick, 45–46
Scooter With Boiling Water Kick, 45
Scooter With Silent Kick, 44–45
Shark, 55
Shoulder Shrug, 57
Silent Kick, 44
Single To Double Arm Pull, 76
Sit And Kick, 51–52
Sitting And Floating Scull, 63–64
Sit-Ups, 134, 140
Snake Wriggle, 72–73
Soap-Slide, 111
Sitting Start, 87
start, backstroke, 100–101
start, breaststroke, 94–95, 96
start, butterfly, 94–97
start, freestyle, 85–89
Straight-Arm Pullovers, 134–135
Straight-Arm Push, 142
Straight Line Checker, 112
Swim Breaststroke, 67
Swimmer's Push-Ups, 134

Tear And Reach, 117–118
Tightening The Pivot, 117
Toe Rise, 136
Towel Stretch, 145
tune-up, 120–121
turn, backstroke, 110–112
turn, breaststroke, 115–118
turn, butterfly, 115–118
turn, freestyle, 104–107
Two, One, Two, 78–79
Up-Stretch, 65
V In/V Out, 79–80
Waiter Kick, 56
Waiter Whip Kick On Back, 63
Waiter Treading Water, 67
Waiter With Dolphin On Back, 78
Wall-Leaner, 143
warm-up, *see specific strokes*
Water-Ski Jump, 56

energy, 151–152, 170

false start line, 160
feet, *see* forces, propelling
flags, backstroke, 160
float, front, 25–26
follow-through, 33
food, 150, 170
forces, propelling, 29–34
  direction of, 32
  line of, 30–32
freestyle
  pull, 31–32
  start in, 85–92
  turn in, 104–107
  see also forces, propelling

grab start, 89–92
graph, *see* charts

hands, *see* forces, propelling

health, 169–171
hydroplaning, 28

judges, 160

kick
  backstroke, 50
  breaststroke, 22, 23, 60
  butterfly, 70
  dolphin, 30, 70
  flutter (front crawl), 20–22, 30

lane lines, 159
lane markers, 159–160

meet, swimming, 159–167
  dual, 147
  invitational or championship, 147
  see also competition; officials; pool, swimming; race
momentum, transfer of, 32–33

officials, 160–162
overloading, 47

pool, swimming, 159–160, 161
  familiarization with, 156
pull, freestyle, 31–32
push-out, pool, 24–25

race, 162–167
recovery, 33–34
referee, 160
rope, practice with, 31–32

rotation, hip-and-ankle, 23–24

sacrifices, personal, 172–173
seeding, 147
shoulder, 20, 143–145
speed, 28
splits, 162–164
sprints, timed, 157
starter, 160
starts, 83
  backstroke, 97–101
  breaststroke, 93–96
  butterfly, 93–97
  forward, 83–97
  freestyle, 85–92
swims, broken, 121–122

teeter-totter principle, 28
tests
  angle of flotation, 25–26
  flexibility, 20–24
  one-in-a-million, 25
  strength, 24–25
training, 36–39
  dry land, 131–145
  interval, 121–123
  water, 120–129
tuck-float position, 25
turns, 103
  backstroke, 108–112
  breaststroke, 112–118
  butterfly, 112–118
  freestyle, 104–107

winning, 165

ABOUT THE AUTHORS

DR. DON VAN ROSSEN is a nationally recognized authority in the field of aquatics. He has a background of thirty years' experience as a successful coach—twelve years in age-group swimming programs and eighteen years as head coach of the University of Oregon swim team. For the past several years, he has conducted workshops for swimmers and coaches throughout the United States and in Mexico.

Dr. Van Rossen has served as chairman of the Aquatic Council of the American Association of Health, Physical Education and Recreation, and as chairman of the Planning Committee for the National Cooperation in Aquatics. He is a past chairman of the Swimming and Diving Rules Committee and the present secretary and editor of the *Swimming Rule Book* of the NCAA.

BARBARA WOODRICH credits the years her three children spent in age-group swimming as important in helping them become productive, self-confident young adults.

Besides swimming and writing for young people, she enjoys horseback riding, sailing, and life on the ranch that she and her husband share with a large assortment of animals.

ABOUT THE ILLUSTRATOR

TOM KELLY is a busy young artist and partner in a Eugene, Oregon design studio. After receiving his degree in fine arts from Whitman College, he spent three years teaching art in Africa. He and his wife and two children live in the country and spend most of their free time on bicycles and skis.

ABOUT THE PHOTOGRAPHER

ANDY WHIPPLE, a Eugene-based freelance commercial photographer, lists his favorite activities as photography, outdoor sports, and music, in that order. He and Tom Kelly have worked together on a wide variety of projects.